HAPPINESS

YOUR 7 MIND POWERS

How To Realize
Your Inner Power,
Believe It, Accept It,
Take Ownership
And Use It To Achieve
Happiness

Diaz Productions LLC

Published by Diaz Productions LLC
1022 North Jefferson Street
St George, UT 84770
http://www.mindfulnesshappiness.com

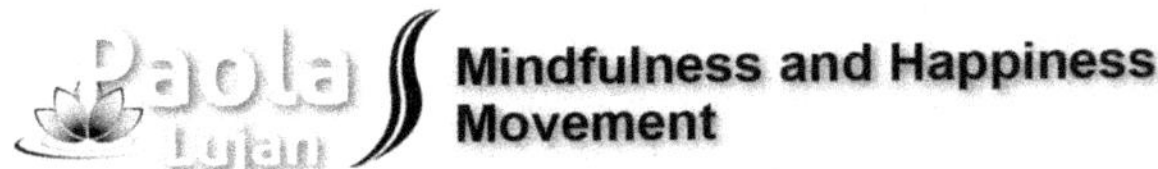

Find us on Facebook here:
https://www.facebook.com/MindfulnessHappiness

****

For weekly tips on how to achieve happiness, inspirational content, and one eBook for free, go to this link and get instant access.
http://www.MindfulnessHappiness.com

****

ISBN-10: 1-943029-00-8
ISBN-13: 978-1-943029-00-6

Disclaimer

Our intention is to help you bring out your biggest dreams and take the first steps to make them a reality. As stipulated by law, we do not make any guarantees about the results you'll get with our ideas, information, tools, or strategies. Your results are completely up to you and the action you take. We believe in you and we are here to support you in making the changes you want for your life while giving you methods, strategies, and ideas that will help move you in the directions of your dreams. The ideas or advices in this book are not intended to replace any professional medical assistance. In fact, users are advised to seek professional medical assistance in the event that they are suffering from any medical problem.

Table of Contents

Acknowledgments

I WANT TO express my gratitude to our Creator for all of the experiences I have in my life, because those make me evolve as a soul.

I would like to especially thank my parents, my first and best teachers, and my brothers who share with me a very important part of my life. I want to recognize the motivation from my extended family and dear friends for all of the love they express.

Finally, I would like to mention my spouse, who is the perfect support and source of inspiration, and my son David, who is my constant motivation to make a difference, so he can have a better world to live in.

Introduction

MY INTENTION WITH this book is to help people change their beliefs about life and realize what they are capable of accomplishing, so they can create that wonderful life they have always wanted. This will be the first of a "make a difference" series of books that will be easy to read and understand, and that will change lives and generations to come.

The concepts and ideas shown in this book are based on research done over the course of 30 years, plus the experiences I have had in my own learning and healing processes. The complete list of the sources and multimedia programs researched is at the end of this book. I encourage you to give yourself the opportunity to read and listen to them; a little at a time will make a huge impact in your life.

I realize that we all learn day after day, month after month, and year after year, thus we change and evolve. I emphasize this because I am writing about all the knowledge I have received up until now. Can this evolve in my next book? Of course! It is part of accepting that there is not just one, and only one, answer to each question in life. We live in an enormous universe with endless possibilities, and the big reason for suffering for most of us is that we want to be right all the time; we want to own the only truth without admitting that what we see is our interpretation of our own reality and not anybody else's reality.

This amazing journey of transformation started in an effort to improve my own life many years ago. At first, I was very reluctant to share it with anyone. I thought, "Who cares? Those were my experiences, how can this help anybody?"

I was wrong. Through years of witnessing human pain, I noticed people often said it was a relief to know they were not alone in their tribulations. It was comforting for them to know that somebody overcame challenges; thus they can recover hope and the courage to go on through those difficult times, simply knowing there is a better future waiting for them; *a future created by them*.

It has been five years since I felt the need to write this book. I first thought that maybe somebody else could write my story, but then I realized that I had the responsibility of sharing my own growth processes; from being the very shy, unhealthy, and fearful girl that I was to being the woman I am today that is eager to tell the world that if I could do it, everybody can do it.

Every person can reach their wildest dreams, if they follow their calling in life and if they are persistent and brave enough to try several times until they achieve the lives they want and deserve.

This book has many purposes. One is to encourage the readers to think "outside the box," to at least consider that life is not just their current routine.

The second purpose is to let them know that they are not alone when they wonder if there is any reason for their existence and if they could someday achieve happiness. I can assure you that if you are reading this book, it is because you are looking for more, the best part is that there are many people like us. Right now, many souls are "awakening" and achieving mindfulness and happiness.

The third purpose is to help people stop unnecessary suffering, bring hope to them, and show them how to get out of that deep emotional pain that seems to be eternal. I want to help, because I know from experience what it feels like to be in misery; that horrible place that seems like a nightmare you want to escape from. It can feel like you want to run but there is no place to go, no place to hide from your pain. For some reason, this can seem to repeat over and over again with a never ending suffering and we wonder...

Why?

Why is this happening to me?

How can I end this pain?

How can I enjoy life?

This misery I mention could be any hard situation that you face; depression, insecurities, anxiety, feeling alone, grief, job loss, not finding true love, not fitting in, broken marriages, dealing with your past, or just feeling that there is something that is missing in your life. This feeling is independent of social status, fame, material possessions, wealth, civil status, age, beauty or the country you live in.

I know what it is like to be desperate and hopeless. I had to face very serious car accidents, broken relationships, cancer and other illnesses plus several surgeries, bankruptcy and a miscarriage to name a few principal events.

What kept me standing was faith and belief; belief that my Creator had something special for me.

Doesn't matter what place you are in now, there is hope, as long as you are willing to take action.

Shall we start?

1

What is Happiness?

"Happiness depends upon ourselves".

– Aristotle: Greek Philosopher and Scientist

WE CAN FIND several definitions in dictionaries, encyclopedias, and, of course, everyone has their own definition of happiness.

A better question is; what is happiness to you? This can be a private question and whatever answer you choose is perfectly fine. Allow me to share my definition of happiness after I explain some ideas.

A Baby is Born

As humans, we are taught that we need somebody to make us happy. This is where the search for that special person who is "supposed to make us happy" begins. It is true that we are individuals who are created to be social; we need that closeness to other human beings. From our early days, we enjoy the company of family and friends; this is undeniable. Since we feel very good being around them, we assume that *they* make us happy.

When we were babies, our caregivers helped us to survive. There is no doubt that without somebody to provide food, clothing, care, protection and shelter, a baby can't survive. What we also receive when we are nursed, is love and that can make us feel good. As we grow up, we become more independent and we don't need anybody to take care of us like when we were babies. Meanwhile, we get less attention from people, yet we still feel that we need somebody else to make us happy because that's the way it used to be.

The Inner Happiness

For years, I thought that I needed a boyfriend to make me happy. When I finally got a boyfriend, after a while, I still felt that something was missing in my life. Then, I thought that when I finished my studies at the university, I was going to be happy later; when I get a well-paying job, when I marry and then when I had my children. The list of "when... I'll be happy" never ended.

It wasn't until a few years ago that I realized I was trying to chase happiness, and what I got in return was an inner conflict. Then, something magical happened; I discovered it. I'd finally figured it out!

Everything I was looking for was inside me.

This discovery was not new, yet it was the first time I made it my truth. This concept has been the subject of many movies, books, and even religions. I had listened to this before, but, at that time, I was not ready to face it. My understanding and love for myself were focused on the exterior rather than inside me.

I was not listening to myself.

All I was doing was trying to fit into the model society that was dictating how things "should be" in order to "be a successful person." I was listening to them and denying my own nature.

I was always attached to somebody else's happiness model. For instance, I always dreamt about a very well-paying job; one that had me working Monday through Friday from 9:00 am to 5:00 pm. In all these years, I actually had only one job, part-time, and that job lasted only 4 months. All the other jobs I ever had were counted as self-employment, even when I was in Peru, my original country. This means that I struggled with my job for over 16 years, wishing things were different. Now, I finally understand that there was a reason why I couldn't find my "perfect job." If I had that "perfect job," I am sure I would have never dared to question anything about my beliefs, because I would have been in my comfort zone. For that reason, now I consider that "lack" as a blessing.

Why is true lasting happiness inside us? Because nothing external is permanent; every moment of praise and recognition for our achievements will pass. The pride to have and to show the world material possessions is ephemeral and parties can't last forever. Even vacations and travels must come to an end.

The only permanence is you. The only person who is always with you 24/7 is you!

In the last few decades, we can find people who have enjoyed wonderful careers and achieved amazing fortunes through their great talents, yet there is still a missing piece from their happiness. They feel alone, without love and appreciation for who they really are. Not just the character they interpret as a music star or a great actor but as a real person with virtues and errors that is yearning to be accepted just the way they are. Sadly, we see them having problems with addictions, unhealthy relationships, or family difficulties to the point that some even take their own lives, because it has been too painful for them to live with themselves.

The Pain of "Being Me"

I can see a lot of pain in some people's eyes when they can't live with themselves. The only individual that you can't escape from is yourself, and the sad part is that, a lot of times, we don't like ourselves. *I know it, I've been there.* I still have some aspects of my personality or my body that I want to change. The difference now is:

I learned to love myself the way I am now.

Yes, I can still change, brighten, and improve some features in me. The key here is that I don't reject or disqualify myself as I used to do it. I have finally accepted the fact that I am a creation of a Superior Intelligence, and that I am doing my best to learn from experiences and to help others. I express gratitude for everything I receive, even challenges because they help me to grow as person, and I really hope for the best, knowing the universe will take care of things I can't control.

My Definition of Happiness

A state of inner peace where I can truly enjoy myself while knowing that I am in control of my thoughts, words, and actions, feeling free to express who I am with love and gratitude, sharing time with my loved ones, and being open to receive love and all good things the universe has for me.

I learned that I can still feel happiness even though my life is not perfect, even if I face some challenges.

I am a happy woman now.

You Can Be Happy Now

Yes, you read that correctly; you can be happy now. Why? Because being happy is a *choice* that you can make.

Does it mean that you will be laughing all the time? Or, that you will never face a challenge? No. It just means that for every situation you face, you can decide how you are going to act, instead of merely reacting all the time as we have been trained to do since we were children.

Confused? Don't worry; let's take one step at a time.

You can have inner happiness, even if your life is not perfect. Again, the only one who can decide to work within yourself is you and only you.

Are you ready to be happy now?

2

It's All About Love

"You yourself, as much as anybody in the entire universe, deserve your love and affection"

—- Buddha: Buddhism founder.

IT IS NO coincidence that the word *love* appears several times in the definition of happiness of every person. If we analyze what we truly seek in life, love is something we can take within ourselves the day we finish our time here on Earth. If you think of any material possession here, there is absolutely nothing we can take with us once our bodies die, except love.

Love can manifest in multiple ways. For instance, patience is love, compassion is love, forgiveness is love, and being there for somebody is love.

We All Want & Need to Be Loved

We all need to be loved, accepted, and we need to feel that we belong or fit into a group. This is part of us.

Dr. William Glasser, author of *Choice Theory*, states, "we are driven by our genes to satisfy five basic needs: survival, love and belonging, power, freedom and fun. In practice, the most important need is love and belonging, as closeness and connectedness with the people we care about is a requisite for satisfying all of the needs." [1]

As a child, friend, spouse, parent, part of a big extended family or as a community member, what we look for first is to be loved. The point here is, what is the meaning of being loved for us? This depends on what we have learned from our environment.

For some people, love is when a person demonstrates with acts that he/she cares for you, that they have your best interest in mind and respect your right to choose. Love is when he/she tells you how much you are loved, and of course, you also need the physical demonstration through hugs, kisses and cuddles.

One of the biggest issues with this, is that people in the past were very reluctant to demonstrate love with words and even more with hugs and kisses. I remember listening to older people say that their mothers disliked kisses and hugs because, for them, love was being obedient. It's no wonder why, in some degree, we feel hungry for love, since most of our grandparents and parents only demonstrated love through

---

1 Dr. William Glasser, The William Glasser Institute http://www.wglasser.com/the-glasser-approach

satisfying needs of survival and being kind, without telling others that they loved them nor giving people the physical demonstration of love.

Our Societal Definition of Love

Unfortunately, for most people, love means that they can take absolute control of you. They think, "if you love me, you have to do what I say." Those are the ones that want to be with you 24 hours a day, 7 days a week when you are just dating. They suppose that, "if you really love them," then you don't need anybody else in your life, and all your time should be spent with them *because that, to them, is "true love."* They want to exercise their power on you, taking away your right to choose freely.

Living in our current society teaches us, mostly throughout the media, a sad definition of love where we lose our right to choose. On the other hand, we are also taught that we should have absolute control and power over our loved ones. From this comes jealousy, selfishness, envy, anger, manipulation, bribery, blackmail, meanness, and suffering, to name just a few.

The big questions are:

Is it possible to enjoy that kind of "love" and not feel asphyxiated?

Do you think you can be happy feeling manipulated or controlled at all times?

Or...

Do you believe you can feel peace knowing that your loved one makes things out of your manipulation or to avoid hurting your feelings rather than from his/her heart?

Fear

After doing meticulous research, analyzing historical characters and observing people that I have contact with, I conclude: *that unhappy and unloved people act from fear.*

Fear that you can replace their love with a new one, fear that you can lose interest in them, or that you don't have enough love for them if you show love for somebody else, as a friend or even family.

As in every aspect of life, everybody has their own opinion, and that is okay. I am not judging you or anybody else since, at some point in my life, I also acted from fear. We all have fear; the difference is how we manage that fear.

Somebody Love Me Please!

We are born with a lot of love inside us. We come to Earth with a full, open heart to give and receive love. *That's our nature and who we are.*

When I was a little girl, I was told that only good girls

are loved. The others, the ones who don't behave as they are supposed to, nobody will love them. Of course I wanted to be loved, and if that meant that I needed to be extremely obedient in order to be loved, then so be it! I didn't allow myself to get dirty. I even deprived myself of playing with other children, because if I soiled my clothing, I thought I was going to be punished, and that was something that I wanted to avoid at all cost. I want to clarify that I never received any wild beating or anything even close to that. Although, I was often reminded what was expected from me. The sole idea of being disapproved of by my loved ones was unbearable for me. The very few times that I was punished verbally while I was a little girl, I felt like I committed a crime and I deserved the worst of hardships. Maybe I was too aware at an early age of what was going on, perhaps too responsible, or for some reason that was one of my gifts and, at that time, I was not capable of understanding it. For so many years, I regretted the fact that I lost the opportunity to behave like a little child, without worrying about anybody else and to just be happy. I never allowed myself that behavior.

Today, I can see that all I was looking for was *love,* and I thought the only way to get it was to please others all the time, even at my childhood's expense. Something that I understood years later, was that my loved ones gave me all the love they could, and what they told me was never intended to hurt me, but to teach me to behave in the same way that they were taught. I didn't know that even if I was not a "good girl," they would still love me. I truly believed that the only way to be loved was to be perfect.

Love Yourself First

In order to receive love from other people, we need to love ourselves first. This concept is not based merely on vanity or egotism but in pure love that we can feel for ourselves when we respect and honor the marvelous creations that we are.

Deepak Chopra totally captured my attention when he said, the amount of love we can feel from the outside is exactly the amount of love we have for ourselves[2].

How come we don't love ourselves? Someone could say, "of course I love myself, I buy the best clothing and jewels for me, I have a beautiful car, I have a lovely hairstyle and my nails are always in perfect shape, what do you mean I don't love myself?" All of those things are based on our ego. We think those things make us happy and we use them as a social mask to hide what is inside us. Those things can be included as bonuses when we really love ourselves; however, if we focus just on those things, we will never feel complete happiness.

I believe the root of that problem is that since we were babies, we were told what we should think, do, feel,

---

2 Arielle Ford, The Art of Love Relationship Series 2014

speak, and how we should behave in order to be the "perfect" child, parent, spouse, neighbor, and so on.

As much as we try, we will never fit into that "perfect model" that was imposed to us, and now we are the ones that continually remind us how "imperfect" or "incapable" we are.

Since we need love and are unable to love ourselves, we look for that love in other people, looking for all that attention, consideration, understanding, respect, company and patience we don't give to ourselves.

But guess what? We are able to receive other people's love up to the same level we can love ourselves. I'm not talking about superficial "love" or selfish love. I'm talking about self-acceptance and loving ourselves as we are. If we don't have that love for ourselves, it doesn't matter how hard other people try to show love for us, it will never be enough.

Not only that, but it is like we have a "shield" against good feelings from other people towards us; we destroy all attention, consideration, understanding, respect, company, and patience that was intended to be for us because, deep inside, we feel unworthy of them. Unconsciously, it is like we are punishing ourselves, rejecting any good feeling from outside.

However, since we can't recognize that all that suffering is coming from inside us, we blame the people around us, sometimes people that love us dearly, because "they don't make us happy." That is the breaking point, because people can feel our energy, can feel our judgment, and, if they can, they will go somewhere else where they will feel appreciated instead of guilty. It is a vicious cycle we weave for ourselves.

This cycle just generates more suffering, and there can be a time when we feel there is no point in living anymore. There can be a time when we don't have any more strength to go on. There can also be a time when we find no reason to be alive, and feel that it would be better for us if we could end the pain of living like this.

I know that, because I have been there and I understand that there is no bigger pain than realizing you don't like and love yourself, that you can't live with yourself. This unbearable pain can lead some people to be involved in alcohol, drugs, and other addictions in order to forget, at least for a little while, the burden they carry and "who they think they are".

I say, "Who they think they are," because that terrible opinion they have about themselves is not who they really are. Every one of us is intelligent, beautiful, amazing, magnificent, and comes with an unlimited potential to shine as a light to the world, and accomplish the mission we came to perform.

3

You are the Protagonist of your Own Movie: You have a purpose in life and you are perfect for it!

"Every human is an artist. The dream of your life is to make beautiful art."

– Don Miguel Ruiz: Mexican Author, Toltec Spiritualist

Our Own World is Like Our Own Movie

We create our own reality based on either what we love or what we hate, depending on what we focus on. Therefore, we are the scriptwriter, the producer, and the main character of our personal story, our personal movie.

Based on that, we think that everything that happens is because of us, both the good and the bad. If our friend is not happy, we think that she is upset with us, and we torture ourselves about what we might have done wrong. If somebody makes a comment we don't like, we feel alluded immediately and react defensively. We get offended if we see somebody that knows us and doesn't greet us. We feel hurt, ignored and get angry about the situation. We take everything personally and it is always "the other person's fault."

As adults, we don't always have Mom and Dad who can tell us what we did wrong. Instead, we now judge, criticize, victimize, and punish ourselves[3]. Before everybody else's eyes, we will always defend our points of view. When we are alone, we treat ourselves as our worst possible enemies. We know our weaknesses and we hurt deeply; we can't forgive our minimal mistakes. We then react with guilt, shame, anger, and other emotions that make us feel miserable.

We all have our own movies and everybody else has a secondary paper; our spouses, children, parents, friends, and every other person in our lives.

Listening to Don Miguel Ruiz[4], I learned that we are the protagonists of our story. Pondering that concept, I had a sublime moment when I realized that since I

---

3 Don Miguel Ruiz, *The Four Agreements, 1997* Chapter 1 Domestication and the Dream of the Planet.

4 Jennifer McLean, "Healing with the Masters" 13th volume, interview to Don Miguel Ruiz

am the main character in my own movie, if I change, the whole story will change.

When I change my thoughts, I change my movie script, thus changing my attitude towards myself and the rest of my environment. Since everybody else is a second character and *I am* the creator of the movie, *I can* have whatever I want in my movie. *I can* change my whole movie and, by consequence, the end of it. I can have the happy ending I always dreamed about.

Nobody Will See the World As You See It

I remember when I was 20 years old, I used to share with dear friends and talk about several things. We were "trying to fix the world." In the conversations, some could see the same situation from different perspectives. I recall that some of us were pretty upset because we could not understand how "they couldn't see it since it was so clear" and, of course, we all wanted to be right.

When I remember that time, I laugh a lot. In the last 20 years, I learned that nobody will see the world as I see it. Even if they want to, they can't, for they are not me. It is as simple as that. They have not lived what I lived, they didn't have the experiences I had. Likewise, we can't force anybody to see the world as we see it.

Now I realize that the most painful experiences are the most valuable for me because they helped me to grow. They helped me to understand how huge the power of belief is, how big the love we can feel from people around us is, and how important it is to give back the same pure love. Maybe we won't give back to the same people that helped us, maybe other people will need love, service, or favor. The important thing here is that we need to help and love others when they need it too.

You Have a Purpose in Life

We are in this human life with a special purpose and for that, we were given special skills and gifts.

A beautiful way to explain this is what I found in the movie Hugo[5]. The protagonist says, he likes to think that the world is a big machine, and in a machine, all the pieces have a purpose. There are no spare pieces, and the machine has a precise number of pieces. He wanted to think of himself like a piece with a purpose, that he was not just a spare piece.

We all have a purpose in life, something we were born to do, a mission. We are not here by accident or by mistake. We fulfill a role in the time and space we are in. Everything we do has a result, whether we like it or not. Indeed we are the result of what our ancestors did before us.

Joe Vitale said, we are like the musicians in an

5 Hugo , 2011
http://www.paramountmovies.com/hugomovie.html

orchestra[6]. Every one of us is necessary and has a part to play in the whole piece of the music we will perform. The orchestra has an exact number of musicians. Now, let's imagine my role is to play the violin, but I am playing the piano. Not only am I not going to be good at the piano, but I am going to screw up the sound that is supposed to be coming from the orchestra. When I play my part, everything flows and I am happy, because I am in a state of bliss.

There is an importance in being clear about what our role is. We will talk about that in the next few chapters.

You Are Perfect the Way You Are for Your Main Purpose in Life

You have a perfect body[7]. The first time I read this I thought, "could that be possible? But I wanted to be taller!" After that, I started observing myself and other people and my conclusion is, yes, we are perfect just the way we are, perfect to accomplish our mission in life.

You may ask, "if we are perfect for our purpose in life, why is that we feel so inadequate, so powerless, and reject ourselves?"

---

6 The Missing Secret Program, Joe Vitale, Session 6: The Power of Zero Limits

7 Don Miguel Ruiz, The Mastery of Love, Chapter 10 Seeing with Eyes of Love

It is because of the way we were trained since we were born.

When we were babies, we lived happily with no knowledge of right or wrong. We had no idea about what was accepted as beautiful or ugly. We didn't know what was considered success or failure. We were simply driven by our natural instincts and we trusted our feelings. If we liked something, we enjoyed it. If we didn't like it, we stayed away from it.

Then, little by little, we lost that ability because we were taught by our parents, siblings, family members, caregivers and teachers what was accepted in our culture as right, wrong, beautiful, ugly, successful, failing, etc., and we believed them.

At first we questioned, "why?" Most of the time, the answers were "because it is!" until we stopped questioning at all, and we accepted what we were taught, assuming it was the "truth."[8] Our culture told us how a man is supposed to look, how a woman needs to have a perfect sculpted body to be considered pretty, what possessions we are supposed to have in order to "fit in," how much money you need to make to be part of the people considered successful, and so on and so on. At the end of all this "learning," we were stuffed with other people's values, ideas, and "truths"

---

8 Loral Langemeier and Bob Proctor, Expression of your Power Live out Loud- Expression vs.Suppression, Cd 1

that rarely were in harmony with our own values, ideas and truths.

As a result, we think we need to please the people we love, so we can receive love in return. We learned that in order to please our loved ones, we have to be as perfect as we can to fit within their values, ideas, and truths. When we were growing up, we struggled with ourselves, because even though we tried really hard, we could not be perfect.

As adults, we were so reinforced with those concepts day after day and year after year that we didn't need the presence or judgment of our caregivers anymore. We became the ones judging ourselves at all times, telling ourselves how "not good enough" or "how inadequate" we were at any given time. In fact, we learned to be very hard with ourselves and made it extremely difficult to forgive ourselves for our own mistakes.

The Drama

Drama makes our self-image very poor, and we conclude that we deserve to be punished; we deserve to be treated badly. We convince ourselves that we are not worthy of love, and we can never reach anything we want in life simply because we don't make a good enough effort and we haven't earned anything yet.

At this point, we even suffer for things that we can't control. Stature can be a prime example. During my teenage years, I complained and disliked the fact that I had a low stature. When I was 15 years old, I went to the endocrinologist in an effort to find a way to grow a little bit more. Tests showed that I was not going to grow much more, if at all. I was then so disappointed and disgusted with how short I was. Let's face it, 5 foot tall describes a short person. On top of that, my nose was not fitting into the "perfect model" and I was slightly overweight. I lost a few pounds and reached a normal weight but I was obsessed with a perfect body. By the time I was 20 years old, even though my weight was 95 pounds, I still struggled with the idea of the perfect body. I exercised using aerobics at home for at least 1 hour every day, sometimes 2 hours. After that, whenever I could, I went to the gym and worked with weights. Despite all of those efforts, I looked in the mirror and looked awful to myself, because I was not "perfect." What I didn't realize at that time was that I truly believed I was ugly, so, no matter what I did, I was going to look ugly to myself. I hated myself for not being perfect, and I concluded that I was not lovable because I was not pretty enough, not tall enough, and not good enough. Sound familiar?

The Truth

The beautiful truth is that we are perfect the way we are for what we were sent here for, for our purpose in life. Yes, after all I have experienced, learned, and overcome, I mean it.

Firstly, all of the perfection models we learned about were somebody else's ideas that very few, if anyone, could reach. If we continually obsessed with those models, all it would bring to our lives is frustration. Even worse, we would constantly compare ourselves to others and would, consequently, always lose.

Secondly, we are individuals with specific characteristics, talents, gifts, and preferences. It is very ingenuous to think that we can all just fit into "one mold."

Thirdly, everybody is designed for their callings, even people with physical limitations. To illustrate this more, let me share some stories.

- Some of the most successful comedians I know are not very handsome, and they are aware of that, yet with just one single grin, they are able to tell the most hilarious jokes and make a lot of people laugh. Basically, they use that fact as a tool to be more funny.

- It is well known that people who can't see develop special sensitivity of their other senses, so that they can compensate that lack. Jose Feliciano, a well known composer and singer who amazed the world for decades with his music, is blind. He plays many musical instruments and can speak several languages. When asked "what makes you happy?" he declared, "waking up in the morning and being grateful for everything God's given me[9]."

- The most touching example, for me, is Nick Vujicic. He was born without arms and legs and he struggled while he learned how to live a life without limitations. According to Nick, the victory over his struggles, as well as his strength and passion for life today, can be credited to his faith in God. Today, this dynamic young evangelist has accomplished more than most people achieve in a lifetime. He's an author, musician, actor, and his hobbies include fishing, painting, and swimming[10]. He is a motivational speaker and author of "Life without Limits," "Unstoppable," "Limitless" and "Stand Strong." His calling in life is to motivate people to change their lives, showing them that if he can be a happy man without arms and legs, they can do it too.

I would like to finish this chapter with three of Nick Vujicic's quotes, which reinforce the idea that you are perfect for your purpose in life. Just recognize your potential and develop your talents, your gifts.

---

9 http://josefeliciano.com/wp/faqs/

10 http://www.lifewithoutlimbs.org/about-nick/bio/

"Dream big my friend and never give up. We all make mistakes, but none of us are mistakes.[11]"

"... for every disability you have, you are blessed with more than enough abilities to overcome your challenges.[12]"

"It's a lie to think you are not good enough. It's a lie to think you are not worth anything."

---

11 http://www.attitudeisaltitude.com/about-nick-his-story

12 http://www.goodreads.com/author/quotes/3395320.Nick_Vujicic

4

Understanding our Origins Nobody can give what they don't have

"Only the one who does not question is safe from making a mistake."

– Albert Einstein: Physicist and Philosopher of Science

ALLOW ME TO make some reflections about us as humans.

After Survival

In nature, we are the only species that search for happiness. Other species focus on survival, evolve, and react to make sure they can leave the next generation. They live by self-preservation. They don't reflect about what they do, they just exist.

Humans, on the other hand, are here to be happy. That is our core, our desire, and ultimately, our right and destiny. We can transcend over generations. We have a wonderful mind that can think, dream, imagine, create, and much more. That is the main reason why we dominate over other species.

It is sad that few people dare to think about happiness and even less try to reach it. In most cases, we behave like other species that just try to survive. People who think outside the box are sadly seen as the "weird" ones who are then punished, bullied, and treated like crazy people.

The "normal" ones are those that live as they are "supposed to." They go to school and work every day in a job they hate, marry, raise children, then retire and die...right? Says who?

Do you really think that we own that unlimited potential and privileged mind just to survive?

If all of mankind had thought that way, we could not have progressed. All of the technology we enjoy today would not be possible; it would not exist.

Have you noticed that humans are the only ones who need beauty in their lives? We feel the need to express our soul through visual arts, music, writing, theater, games, etc. We are the only living creatures on Earth that need to believe in a Higher Intelligence, thus we have religion.

For years, scientists and archaeologists have found

legacies from our ancestors in the forms of paintings, sculptures, carved stones, decorated pottery, monuments, writing, scientific records, architecture, etc. These are expressions of their souls, the need that they had to leave something for their descendants, so they can build upon them. As far as I know, for any other species on Earth, all we can find are bones and remains.

In this moment, as I am writing, I am doing it from my heart and for a deep need to express what I think and what I have learned that helped me to be at peace with myself. This is so that I can teach my descendants, and people who are willing to read, how to reach happiness and possibly avoid the mistakes I have made.

For generations, we had behaved like other species, just trying to survive. We never stopped to think, ponder or meditate. Everything we did and continue to do is in auto-pilot. Have you noticed that once you master a task, you don't even think to execute it anymore? That happens when we drive, when we dress, when we brush our teeth, when we work, etc.

I believe that is a wonderful characteristic of ours; for some tasks, we don't need to think anymore. However, when we are not used to reflecting about anything at all, we face several risks.

The first risk is getting trapped in the false belief that you can't be different or, even worse, if you are different, then you are in trouble. History shows that the most remarkable and prolific inventors of our time were very curious and were eager to learn and explore. However, they were usually labeled by our society, because society couldn't understand their wonderful mind since they were different. Luckily for us, they didn't give up and always had somebody who motivated them while believing in their talents.

The second risk is losing your ability to dream. When we are in "automatic mode," we don't even think about what we want. We just follow rules and kind suggestions from people that want to help us but they can't teach us what they don't know. If you are not clear about what you want for your life, then life will give you whatever comes first. Generally, our worst fears tend to manifest. In order to achieve what we want, first we need to know what it is. This can be pretty obvious, but difficult to be clear about.

The third risk is never inquiring about the path we are taking. When life is so dynamic and time is so scarce, we don't take a break and wonder if what we are doing to make our living is something we enjoy or not. We don't stop to think about whether or not the path we are taking is the right one for us.

Remember, the answer is always inside you. Nobody can tell you what really makes you happy. People close to you can have a good idea about what you like, but you are the only one who truly knows what makes you happy.

So, why do we stop dreaming? Why do we not know what we want?

It is because we are taught that to dream is useless, that life is hard, because it is the way it should be. We are told that we need to suffer through adversity and pay for our mistakes. Sometimes we consider that we deserve suffering, for we are not the perfect type of person we should be.

Yes, we like to enjoy life's pleasures, and deserve it, but when people struggle with poverty like a lot of the population, when they barely have the resources to survive, how can they even think about enjoying anything? For instance, for a lot of people, going on vacations is a luxury they can't afford. The ones who can take vacations usually come back and say something like, "oh, I have to return to my sad reality now." We come back to a life that we don't like, one where if we could change it, it would be very different. We live resigned and face day after day what life throws at us, feeling powerless to change or modify anything.

Well, since I could radically change my life for better, I can say with in-depth knowledge that *you can do it too.*

Did it happen overnight? No; it took about one year before I could implement what I had learned.

Did all challenges in my life disappear? No; I just faced them differently.

Will it take you one year to see results? No; the results depend on many factors, and everybody is unique. The important thing here is to be consistent. You can take baby steps if you want to. Over time, you will see the results.

Can you see results faster? YES! This just depends on how much effort you dedicate to your self-growth and knowing what techniques are appropriate for you, so you can accelerate results.

Was it worth it? YES, it was!

Nothing was the same once I listened to my first self-development program. After years of reading tons of self-help books, which made a difference in my life, I have to say that my first audio program was the one that opened my mind to a better life. Finally, I was ready to change. Finally, I found hope. For the first time in my life, I didn't feel alone. I discovered there was a big group that wondered the same things I wondered, that questioned the same societal rules I questioned. They were achieving the life of their dreams, doing what they were meant to do.

I discovered that there was no need to "suffer" and that if I know what I want, I can create it, for I have the power to create my life.

Indeed, I am creating the life of my dreams, and the best is yet to come!

Nobody Can Give What They Don't Have

It is quite simple; if I don't have water, then I can't give you water, right? If I don't have love, then I can't give you love. I can't respect somebody else if I don't respect myself. Likewise, I give you what I have. If I have fear inside, I will send you fear. It is clear yet difficult to see in our own lives or what we expect from other people, especially our loved ones.

Part of our suffering is that, most of the time, we expect people close to us to be more respectful, understanding, loving or forgiving. If they don't forgive themselves, how can they forgive you? If they didn't receive physical demonstrations of love during their lives, how can they give that to you? They just simply don't have it, and then they can't give it to anyone else.

The Last Four Generations; A Little of our History

When you look back to our ancestors, you can see that their lives were completely different. Our great grandmothers had to look for wood, go to their kitchens, light the fires, and then start cooking after all of that work combined. This goes without saying that many of them cultivated their own vegetables and raised their own poultry. When they had to iron, they needed to light the charcoal to put inside the smoothing iron. On top of that, they had a lot of children to take care of. No wonder they had very little time to give their children all the cuddling and personalized attention they needed; they were exhausted and not in the most cheerful of moods.

Back then, our grandmothers couldn't receive much education; they could hardly ask for any answers. If they dared to argue any societal rules, they were severely punished. The punishments needed to be so hard, or so their parents thought, so that they would remember it very well and never repeat the same mistakes again. Many times, they were told to shut up and be quiet because that is how "good girls" behave. The more submissive and quiet they were, the better.

This is how they learned from generations to hide their emotions and hate themselves because of their mistakes. Every time they had a painful emotion, they masked it because they were not allowed to cry or demonstrate any sign of trouble, discomfort or frustration. These were seen as being for weak people, and weakness labelled them as shameful. We know that emotions are energy; imagine how much repressed energy they had inside. They didn't know how to deal with their emotions and they couldn't face their real fears and feelings, because it was too painful.

When they grew up and married, that is what they taught their children, because it was all they knew, *all they ever received*. How could they be more understanding about the emotional needs of growing children if they struggled to at least fill their own survival needs? Nevertheless, they did all they could, and even more, to give all their love and the best to their children. I think they were superheroes to do everything that they did!

The next generation, our parents, are the result of all that effort, and they were allowed to enjoy even more technology than the previous generation. They were able to use gas and electrical stoves, mixers, blenders, televisions, radio, stereos, telephone, air conditioning, heating, various vehicles, and more. Our mothers spent time with us but they had to work outside the home. This brought more stress to their lives, since they were not released from their duties at home in the meantime. This means that when they returned home very tired after work, they still had to cook, clean, help us with homework, and take care of family matters. It is true that our fathers were involved in home chores and we could feel more closeness than they could feel with their fathers, even though the responsible one for the children and home was still the mother. Our parents could spend more time with us as family and again, *they did the best they could*.

Since their childhood was hard in most cases, our parents tried to provide more comfort for us, so we don't go through what they had to go through and were much less strict with us than the generation before. In fact, I can say that in all my childhood, I didn't receive more physical punishment than a slap once in a while. That doesn't mean I was not corrected when I made mistakes, because I was. It just means that the level of physical violence was substantially less.

Our parents had to face another challenge that before was very uncommon; divorce. Many of my friends have grown up with only one of their parents, and that created another type of conflict. The ideal environment to raise children is a home with a mother and father together. In some situations, that is not always possible. Sometimes, it is much better to have parents apart rather than have children witnessing fights all time. Even in those circumstances, as children, we always want to see mom and dad together, so choosing just one of them affects the personality and emotional stability of the children. As humans, we can get used to a lot of things and as time passes, children adapt to the new parent picture. Inevitably[13], they feel like they are betraying one of the parents when they enjoy time with the other parent. However, since we are taught from our ancestors to hide our emotions, our generation was keeping inside a greater pain that could become unbearable. We pretended everything was good, as if ignoring the situation would make it disappear, but nothing could be further from the truth.

Today, many women have to work and leave their children in daycares, because their parents don't live close. Unfortunately, the number of divorces has increased, meaning that there are more single parents than ever. If raising children was difficult enough

---

13 Utah FosterCare, *On Becoming a Foster Parent Manual,* Class 7 Adoption & Permanency, page 273

for both parents together, single parents have to put in huge amounts of effort to make it work. The number of children in families is less than the generation before, even to the point where just one child is considered enough, or worse, people don't even want to have children anymore.

We have very advanced technology that is present in every aspect of modern society: through our smartphones, computers, laptops, notebooks, video games, media, and more. Children nowadays prefer to play video games rather than go out and play with friends and exercise. We have replaced the warmth of personal relationships with social media and technological networking.

Much time has passed, yet some patterns repeat in our society today:

We are still trained to hide our emotions because we don't want to deal with them, and even if we could recognize when something is wrong, we don't know what to do with it.

Likewise, we have the same nature and need for love as in our beginnings. It is the way we are created; *we are love.*

5

Power 1: The Power of Clarity What Do You Want?

"Anything the mind of man can conceive and believe, it can be achieved."

– Napoleon Hill: American Author

Discover this on a deep level and be totally honest with yourself.

Today I challenge you with this simple yet very revealing question:

What do you want?

I am not talking about what you think you deserve. I am not asking you to be realistic. What do you really, truly want?

The first time I heard this question in "Expression of your Power[14]," I realized that I had lost my ability to dream, so I started to dig deep inside with several questions, meditations, and exercises that helped me remind myself of who I am and what I am capable of achieving.

Like many people, when I started to think about that, I immediately pictured more income, better houses, a new car, traveling, vacations, and so on. However, something inside was asking me, "really? Is that all you really want? That's it?" Let me tell you that I was not judging myself for wanting those external pleasures, it was just the feeling that something was missing.

At that time, I was convinced that what I wanted in life for my career was to own a big bakery with a section for wedding cakes, another for custom cakes, and to be able to sell fine pastries and desserts to eat in a bistro space. I also wanted to establish a baking school and to be able to teach high class decorating skills and sugar flowering for very exclusive, delicate wedding and custom cakes. For the last 8 years, I was teaching and baking professionally every day. I was selling pastries for some restaurants and really enjoying the feeling that I could make beautiful cakes and sugar flowers. In fact, in any free time that I had, all I was looking and searching for in libraries and online was more recipes or new techniques to make the most

---

14 Loral Langemeier and Bob Proctor, Expression of your Power Live out Loud- Expression vs. Suppression Cd 2

exquisite desserts and cakes to please myself, family, friends, and clients. Still, something was missing.

As I searched and asked more, I found this question that was crucial to finding out what I wanted for my life:

What do you enjoy so much that you will do it for free? [15]

The answer was revealing to me. I remembered all the days and hours spent making cakes and even though I enjoyed it, I would not do it for free.

So I thought; all these years of pursuing my dream bakery school, were they for nothing? After investing a lot of money in the business and literally working and learning for thousands of hours, I realized that it was not my purpose in life. At first, I felt pretty disappointed in myself, even to the point of feeling guilty. Then, I could figure out what was going on. I hadn't wasted my time or money; I was just doing the best activity I found (until then) to make my living.

Looking at it from another perspective, in the last 25 years of my life, I was looking for the career that was more satisfying and meaningful to me. First, I graduated as an architect and worked in something I liked. Then, as I moved to the United States of America, I worked as a real estate agent while enjoying the business part of it. Later, I found a better passion, one that

---

15 http://www.automaticincomecoach.com/

filled my need to create beauty with my own hands, and then I started the bakery business. I learned every step of the way, and I did it with passion and commitment. There was nothing to regret, nothing to be ashamed of.

I tried; I know what it is to get an education in a university and graduate. I know what it is to be an associate agent, and I know what it is to own a small business.

So now what? Then what? What is my purpose in life? What is my mission in life? What would really make me feel useful? As days passed, I was looking inside myself, asking myself some transcendental questions while remembering the times when I felt the most happy and energized. I was writing lists of what I liked and disliked, what I would love to do, what I was definitely not willing to do, and then I got it!

For the last 12 years, I have belonged to a women's association where we gather every week to learn and actively participate in classes where we nourish one another. We can share our thoughts and experiences about many topics related to spiritual and personal growth, family, children, and marriage. I have had the privilege of teaching many classes, and, for some periods, led or been a part of the leading group. In this particular association, we help one another whenever a problem arises and support the families in need. We know each other by name, we love the families we network with and make services with.

Then, for a little more than 2 years, at the same time

as being involved with that women's association, I was working with children from 18 months up to 12 years old. In the beginning, it was a little hard, yet when I had to give them a class, it felt really good. I learned to love them and connect with them. I helped them to understand that in 15 more years, or so, they would be the ones who would be in charge; they would be the leaders of the next generation. I believe in motivating children to find their talents and to do the best they can. I don't expect them to be number one in everything they try; I just encourage them to do their best.

I soon discovered that when I was teaching motivational classes, this was when I felt I was doing what I was meant to do. I could feel the energy flowing, the audience enjoyed it, and I was doing it for free! Also, every time I was chosen to give a speech to a bigger and more diverse audience, I felt like I could have done it all day long...for free! At some points, people asked me if they could have my speech in writing as they could feel a connection with my words that helped them understand some issues in their own lives.

Finally, I had found my purpose in life:

> To share what I had learned through experiences, how I could find joy, happiness and peace on the path, and how to solve issues in life that are not supposed to make us suffer, but to learn and understand our life purpose and make the best of it.

With this statement, I don't want you to think my life

is perfect, because it isn't. I still have challenges; I am still working with myself every day. I still have unexpected issues like everybody else, and I still have days where I feel down.

The difference now is that I know what I was sent for, what my reason is for being here. I trust myself and now I count on me to face any challenge in life, because I know I can do it!

How I Found Out What I Wanted

When I started to listen to personal development programs, I had this erroneous idea that my subconscious mind was my enemy, because, from my point of view, it was the part in me that was making me miserable.

Once I understood that my subconscious mind was trying to protect me, I was able to move on. It's interesting that the career I am choosing now was one that, in the past, I never thought I could do at all. Actually, I was completely intimidated and afraid to even try it.

Later, I learned that when something is very important to us, our subconscious mind is going to try to hide it from us in a place that we would never dare to search, because it would be too scary. That was its way of protecting us.[16]

So, how can we discover what is really important to

---

16 Paul Scheele, Abundance for Life Main Course. Prelude Sessions.

us? I am not suggesting that if you have a phobia, you go and face it right away. You can do it if you want; it will open new doors to your life. I had to face my phobia of dogs, and, after I did it with a puppy that my little brother adopted, it was the most special relation to an animal that I could have ever had.

What I am suggesting you take on is the possibility of opening your mind to new activities, to trying new things. If it is not working for you, or if it is not important enough for you to keep trying, it is okay. At least you now know that the activity is not for you.

There was a time when I said, "I could do anything in the world, but to teach, I don't have the patience." Some years later, I proved myself wrong. Same thing with children, I always thought that I could not deal with children, and again, I proved myself wrong.

Those two talents were discovered serving other people. When I joined that women's association, as a leader, I had to teach a lesson every two months. Also, if a teacher was not available for any reason, one of my responsibilities was to teach that week's lesson. The first time, I was thrilled and afraid. However, when I started to teach, something inside me was like a fire, a strong feeling that I was meant to teach. After that first lesson, I noticed that I liked it so much that I was volunteering every time to teach.

Working with children was much more challenging. In the beginning, I was afraid of children. I know it sounds unusual but what scared me was that I couldn't control them. I remember a particular Christmas Day where I was alone with 20 children. It was my second month working with them and I didn't know how to handle the situation. I played a video for them and hid in the bathroom to cry for at least a couple of minutes. Now, as I recall the experience, I laugh a lot.

It took me time to get used to children. Since it was my turn to give back the dedicated and loving service I received, and still receive with my son, *I chose to make it work*. The more I struggled with it, the more difficult it was for me. When I decided I wanted to give all my energy and effort to teach children, that was when I was able to find a good connection and really learned to love them. It is amazing what you can achieve when you love people. It was a pleasure to prepare the lessons, especially to motivate them and let them know that they are our future. I tried to make it fun for them. I learned that children can cooperate gladly with adults if we show respect, interest, understanding and, above all, love. Of course, once I learned my lesson with children, life challenged me with another kind of service. That experience taught me to have a more loving relationship with my son and to break some beliefs I had about parenting.

How to Find Out What YOU Want

1. Go to a quiet place where you feel safe; a place that relaxes you. You can play soft music, if you want. Be alone, so nobody interrupts you.

2. Ask yourself these questions[17]:

   What do I want?

   What is my purpose in life?

   What was I sent here for?

   If you knew you could not fail, what would you do?

   If money wasn't a concern to you, what would you do with your life?

3. Allow your mind to wonder and dream; what desires come to you? Observe what comes to your mind first. Do not judge or change it.

4. *Write down* your ideas and observations.

5. Review your ideas and ask yourself[18]:

   If this could be here TODAY, will I accept it?

If for some reason you wouldn't accept it today, then reconsider if that is what you want.

Your inner self knows. The universe will reveal to you the answer; this answer is, and has always been inside you. Trust your intuition. Everyday, you can make a baby step towards your dream life.

---

17 Rhonda Byrne, Hero Audio Book, Cd 1

18 Paul Scheele, Abundance for Life Main Course. Prelude Sessions. Audio Set 4 - Seven-Step Creative Process of Manifestation

More Ideas in How to Find Out What You Want:

1. Make lists.

   - Make a list of three or five things you like to do. They could be anything. Include your hobbies. (List #1)
   - Make a list of five things you don't like at all. (List #2)
   - Dream, imagine, and ponder about the things you like the most from list #1 and figure out which of the two you would do for free. (List #3)
   - Make a list of what you think are your strengths and abilities. (List #4)
   - Make a list of what other people say you are very good at. (List #5)
   - Find the similarities between lists #4 and #5. This will be your list #6
   - Think about what values are most important to you. (List #7) You can find several websites online with value lists to help you. Here I share with you this website[19] http://www.mindmovies.com/inspirationshow/archive.php?episode=8

---

19 Natalie Ledwell, The Inspiration Show http://www.mindmovies.com/inspirationshow/archive.php?episode=8

- Another good idea is to think about how you would like to be remembered once you are gone.[20] What would you like your family to say about you to their children? Align your dreams with those values, because those are the most important things to you. (List #7)

Now you know:

What you like: list #1

What you don't like: list #2

What you like the most: list #3

Which strengths you own: List #6

Which values are important to you: List #7

This is your starting point. Indulge yourself and recognize the effort you made to find out what it is important to you.

You can add more than five items to any list or they could have less than five items. You are the boss here, you decide.

2. To help you more in discovering what you want, I found this website[21] that raises the following questions to help individuals find what their interests are:

---

20 Sonia Ricotti, Unsinkable Program, Bonus Class

21 http://www.how-to-change-careers.com/new-career-ideas.html

- What do you enjoy doing in your leisure time?
- What would you rather be doing?
- Which of your interests would you most like to pass on to your kids?
- What inspires you?
- What past passions have you lost touch with?
- What did you love doing as a child, as a teenager, when you first started working?
- When have you been so absorbed in something that you lost track of time? What were you doing?
- If you were accidentally locked in a bookshop overnight, which section would you camp out in?
- If you won the lottery and did not have to work for money, what would you choose to do with your time?

Everybody has a unique set of talents, gifts, strengths and skills. Of course, we need to use them in order to master them. The seed is inside you, you just need to nurture it. After your answers come to your heart, I would like to invite you to think, meditate, and ponder about these questions again:

What do I want?

What is my purpose in life?

What was I sent for?

I am sure you will find your answers. They can take time; rest assured that they will come. Let your subconscious mind work on them and when answers come, *write them down as soon as possible,* or you may forget about them. Here is where the fun begins.

Something to Consider

What you like now can change later, and it is okay.

As you try new things or try the ones you think you like, you can discover that you don't like them too much, or that they are not as important as they used to be. Be gentle with yourself. If you find that this applies to anything on your list, it is okay to change it. Be brave and recognize that even if you have talent for that, you don't enjoy that activity anymore.

That happened to me with decorating cakes. As I told my story in previous chapters, I graduated from Architecture and Urbanism in 1998. Let's say that was something I liked; at that moment, that was good. When I moved to the United States of America, I worked as a real estate agent; that was still good. I then discovered a passion that was better for me; I could create and be more artistic with my own hands. I could express the "girly" side of me. This activity was better for me; it was something I did with all my heart. After 8 years, when I finally surrendered to the fact that I needed to share what I had learned that helped me to be happy, that is when I discovered that

I needed to write a book to teach and motivate people. My process was like this:

Architect and Planner	Good
Realtor	Good
Baker and Sugar Artist	Better
Author and Motivational Speaker	Best

Let me confess that the process was not easy. Can you imagine what people said (and thought) when I announced that I was going to bake and decorate cakes instead of continuing with the previous activities? I don't need to write it, you can guess it. To a lot of close people, I was crazy. Others thought that it was a waste of time and that I studied in a university for a higher reason, but not to just bake cakes. I was doing what my heart and soul were telling me to do, and I can tell I enjoyed it so much. However, it took a lot of effort and courage to walk that path. Fortunately, I had the support of my family; they were always there for me.

The path I am taking now is even more "unusual" for most people. I understand it is not an easy one. Nevertheless, I have to try it. It is where my heart and soul are right now. I am writing this, my first book, with passion, with all my heart, and with the clear intention of helping people to be happy, even with everyday challenges. I know it is possible; I experience it in my own life each day.

What I am trying to explain is that it doesn't matter what you like, don't discard it. Between strengths, virtues, values, skills, and talents, you have many of them, and it is not important which category they are in. The important thing is that you own them. Many people think that if they don't dance, sing, perform, or do any artistic work, they don't have talents. Talents and gifts could be anything you are good at, anything you enjoy doing.

Once You Know It...

You will be so excited and happy when you find out what you want that you will desire to share it with the world. Let me give you a word of caution; don't be discouraged by people around you. We all have in our lives our own "Discouragement Committee" and even though they are thinking about our own good, they sometimes can't understand our motives, and that is okay. Remember, nobody can see the world the way you see it. As long as you feel inside that it is what you want to do, go for it; dream and believe you can do it!

6

Power 2:
The Power of Choice
Taking Ownership

"It is our choices... that show what we truly are, far more than our abilities."

*– J. K. Rowling:
Harry Potter's Author*

Our Free Will

We are sent to Earth with a marvelous faculty; our free will. Our free will is our birthright. It is a powerful characteristic of ours that no one can mess with unless we give them that right. We can always choose our actions, but we can't control the consequences of our actions. Ultimately, the one that will face the consequences of your actions is you. So, don't you think you need to choose what you want to do?

Nevertheless, there are always people who believe

that they have the right to tell us what we should do. We live in a society and we have rules that need to be respected in order to live in harmony. I am not suggesting that if you want to rob a bank, you should do it just because that is what you want; not at all.

I recognize that there are countries where people live with dictatorship-style governments, and freedom can be compromised. I am also not suggesting that you should risk your life to speak your mind.

What I am telling you is that we can choose our thoughts and actions pertaining to our lives without messing with other people's free will.

When we are first born, we can't choose anything because we depend completely on others to take care of us. As soon as we are responsible enough for our actions, we choose what actions we take. However, they are very influenced by people around us. By the time we are adults, nobody can force us to think or do anything but we usually don't recognize it that way.

We feel trapped in the "truths" we were taught throughout our lives. Most of the time, those "truths" are not aligned with our desires and our values, thus we have a painful conflict between what we want and what we "should" do to please our loved ones and to be a "good girl /good boy." We feel that we want to rebel against every societal rule, and we can't see why we feel that way. We then feel guilty for having those feelings until the point where we think something is truly wrong with us, and then we feel even more guilty.

Most people are convinced that they don't have a choice in anything. They say that the government, spouses, work, bosses, the law, and everybody else limits their freedom. While they think that way, they will feel powerless to shape their lives and will behave like victims of the circumstances.

Choice Theory

William Glasser, M.D. in The Ten Axioms of Choice Theory states[22]:

> "1. The only person whose behavior we can control is our own."

This is his first Axiom and his Choice Theory is based on that.

"Dr. Glasser's approach is non-traditional. He does not believe in the concept of mental illness unless there is something organically wrong with the brain that can be confirmed by a pathologist"[23]. In the next Axioms he states some definitions of behavior:

---

22 William Glasser, M.D., Choice Theory, 1998, Chapter 13 Redefining Your Personal Freedom.

23 Dr. William Glasser, The William Glasser Institute http://www.wglasser.com/the-glasser-approach

> "8. All we can do from birth to death is behave. All behavior is Total Behavior and is made up of four inseparable components: acting, thinking, feeling and physiology."
>
> "10. All Total Behavior is chosen, but we only have direct control over only the acting and thinking components. We can, however, control our feelings and physiology indirectly through how we choose to act and think."

As we can see, the concept that we can choose is not just a "good idea" but something that was demonstrated by a psychiatrist life's work.

Nowadays, the number of mental illnesses is increasing, and we witness the deterioration of people's minds and that of our society. We can see it in the media, in the movies, in the crimes, and in the wars around the world.

Can we make a difference? Of course we can. If we start with ourselves, choosing our lives and our future, people we are in contact with will benefit from our change, and by helping ourselves, we can make a huge contribution to the world.

Every Day, We Are Choosing

Every day is a new opportunity to start our lives. We can choose if it is going to be a wonderful day, or if it will be a miserable one. This choice is independent if our life is "less than perfect." After all, who has a "perfect life"?

Most people wait until their life is "perfect" to decide what kind of thoughts they will have or what kind of life they want. The "perfect life" is never here, so they think that they never have a choice.

This is not the way it works.

First, we need to make our choices, shape our futures, and then achieve our dream lives. Is it ever going to be perfect? Well, if you mean a "perfect" life without any challenge at all, then no. We all have and will continue to have challenges. It is the way we grow, by overcoming challenges.

Does this mean we are here to suffer? No; it means that we can choose the attitude we will face the challenges with. The better our attitude, the faster we will overcome our challenges, and the best part is, we will learn the lessons needed.

Our Magnificent Power

We have a magnificent power within us; we can choose. We can choose our thoughts, actions and, above all, our behavior. We are responsible for every decision we make and have to live with the consequences of those decisions.

In my research, I have found people who have told me "I can't choose my feelings," or "I have no choice but to live with this person, although he/she abuses me. I have no place to go, I am trapped."

As long as they think that way, it is true. However, they are *choosing* to stay in the same situation. It is their fear that makes them think that they have no choice, but it is not true; they always have a choice.

When we recognize that our beliefs and the way we are programmed, are the ones that make us think we have no choice, we have taken a big step to our freedom. Realize they are just beliefs, they are not true.

This choice power brings not only responsibility, but also ownership; ownership of our behavior and what we can achieve with the endless capacities we are given. We need to recognize our inner power, the day we do that is when our freedom is closer than ever.

7

Power 3: The Power of Your Thoughts Everything is Created Twice

"If you want to find the secrets of the universe, think in terms of energy, frequency and vibration."

– Nikola Tesla: Inventor and Futurist

WE CREATE EVERYTHING twice; first with our thoughts and then it later manifests into our lives[24]. We need to understand that our thoughts are energy and that energy has the ability to shape matter.

Science demonstrated long ago that sound waves in different frequencies modify different mediums like

---

24 Mary Morrissey, Dream Builder Program

the particles of solid elements and liquids[25]. Most of us can hear and enjoy the sound of music, so we know that sounds exist.

Light also has different frequencies, and our eyes can detect just some of them. Nowadays, we have special kinds of cameras that can capture images of things we can't even perceive with our eyes.

What about love? Can you see it? Touch, taste, smell, or hear it? No. Can you feel it? Yes, every time. By love, we are here and have a body. We survived because somebody loved us enough to take care of us when we were babies, otherwise, we would be dead.

Love is energy, a very powerful one.

Our Thoughts are Energy

The beautiful mind that we own has the capacity to generate thoughts. Our thoughts are energy and have different frequency waves. Thoughts vibrate at different frequencies depending how positive or negative they are. If they are positive, they have a high vibration. The opposite happens with negative thoughts.

Thoughts generate feelings and these become magnets, attracting whatever we place our attention on, for the good or for the bad.

---

25 Dr. Hans Jenny, Cymatics experiments, 1960 https://www.youtube.com/watch?v=l4jUMWFKPTY

How Our Brain Works

Scientific studies demonstrate that we see the reality not the way it is, but the way our brain interprets it based on previous experiences[26]. Our wonderful brain is based on patterns, and in order to interpret what occurs, it needs to adjust the facts to previous patterns to make sense or understand what is going on. That means that we "see" a "distorted reality," or explained in another way, we see reality with our own "personal glasses or filters." This is why two people can see the same fact but perceive a different "truth."

I can recall a time when I had a very revealing experience about what I had "perceived."

I was listening to a group coaching call and was waiting on the phone to have the opportunity to talk to the coach. I had talked to her the previous week and she advised me about an issue I had with a person who is very close to me. I was still very stuck in the fact that even though I was capable of recognizing it was my attitude and feelings for that person that made me suffer, I felt hopeless to change it. When I could finally talk to the coach, she nicely advised me to separate my issue with that person from the general negative mindset I had regarding success. She also reminded me to read a book and use some tools in that book to deal with the relationship issue.

---

26 Paul Scheele, Abundance for Life Program. Prelude

Because I had this negative attitude, and felt like a victim, what I had "heard" was that she was mean and ridiculed me. I knew she was right about what she said, but I was hurt and ashamed to listen to the recording. I was thinking, "It was so embarrassing, so many people were in the call and all I could talk about was this issue. That was very stupid of me and since it was recorded, everybody can listen to how stupid I am. I wish I had never called." One month later (yes, it took me four weeks to have the courage), I listened to the call and realized that the coach was never mean to me, nor did she treat me badly. I could feel her interest in helping me with that situation. I couldn't believe that it was the same call, yet indeed it was. I could have saved myself four weeks of embarrassment by just listening to it before!

What happened here? It was how I perceived the call. The fact is what was recorded, and it was my interpretation of the fact that was distorted with my own filters. My attitude towards the issue was negative and I was in victim mode. My brain "stretched" what I heard to fit it into my "negative database" and to make sense of it.

I was very blessed to have the recording this time. However, in other day to day issues, we might not have the same resources. That is how two people manage to see the same scene differently and both are right. They may have "perceived" it that way, but it doesn't mean it is the fact.

The "Real World"

It is undeniable that we live in a universe that has several elements we can't detect with our five senses. However, as humans, we are stubbornly determined that our "real world" is just what we can see with our own eyes and nothing more.

Most people say, "If you can't see, hear, touch, smell, or taste it, it doesn't exist. Stop dreaming and put your feet on the ground; this is the real world and in the real world, we need to pay bills, so go get a real job and bring money to the table!"

Isn't it funny that even though the results we get with a "real job" aren't the ones we want, we still are attached to "the real thing"? Generally, the "real job" generates a "real paycheck" that lasts one week if we are lucky. This job is where we feel trapped and miserable, because we are not doing what we like. Instead, our talents are wasted and battered.

Each time we try another activity that is more rewarding for us, but it doesn't yield the big paycheck at the beginning, people around us are telling us how it is not going to work, and why we need to come back to "the real job." Because of this way, most people lose excellent opportunities to do what they love, because they don't endure enough. They lose the big picture for their illusion of security.

Of course, in the real world, we need to pay bills, but I am not suggesting you quit your job today and pursue your dreams. People who have reached their dreams have planned ahead. Sometimes they start with a company part-time while still working their "real job" to make money and pay the bills. Other times, they were saving some money every month while doing research or taking classes to prepare for their dream life. They worked with their thoughts, they visualized and they stayed positive at least once every day, even in the worst circumstances.

What we need to understand is that energy is real too. Even though we can't see it, it is as real as things you can touch.

Fortunately, science has made huge discoveries in the last few decades that allow us to open our eyes and minds to new facts. If we use them to our advantage, we can create a new life.

How My Thoughts Changed My Medical Bills

Let me share with you a real fact from my life (from within the "real world") that was changed by the power of my thoughts. I used to have large medical bills; at one time, they were as big as $90,000 all together, or even more. After my bankruptcy, they were gone but my health was still poor and I started to accumulate more medical bills. I had three more surgeries, more expensive studies, and more suffering. Within almost four years, I had accumulated around $15,000 more in medical bills.

It has been 2 years since I started to change the way

I feel about my body. I stopped freaking out every time I noticed something unusual and just focused on being healthy, trusting my body to heal itself, being positive, and avoiding all negativity in media and people around me. Instead, whenever I feel a symptom, I know something is bothering me, and it is time to make some changes. Generally, it is because I am taking care of and loaded with problems that are not mine. Other times, I am overdoing tasks and not getting enough rest, nor am I having fun. I learned to listen to my body, to be patient with it, and to have reasonable expectations. Most importantly, I love and accept my body.

Two months ago, I realized that I had no more medical bills! I couldn't believe it, that this was real. Thoughts change matter and beliefs can make a big difference between a healthy body and a sick one.

8

The Magical Wand: Stop the Pain

"Change your thoughts and you change your world".

– Norman Vincent Peale: Author, Professional speaker, Minister

Thoughts, Beliefs, Feelings, Attitude and Paradigms

To re-create your reality, you just have to change your thoughts, that's it! Your thoughts are the starting point for everything.

Let me define some concepts[27]:

- Your thoughts form your beliefs.

27 Loral Langemeier and Bob Proctor, Expression of your Power Live out Loud- Expression vs.Suppression, Cd 1

- Your thoughts generate feelings within you.
- Your beliefs define the attitude you have regarding anything.
- A group of beliefs form a paradigm.
- Paradigms are the "truths" that rule your life.

If you were in an extreme situation and everything was taken from you, nobody could take your thoughts away. There is no way for any person to obligate you to think anything. You can pretend you are doing it, but inside your head, you can think whatever you want and nobody could prove you are pretending.

The only person who can decide what thoughts you'll have is YOU. Based on the definitions explained previously, your thoughts define your attitude.

This means that the person that controls your attitude is you, and it starts in your thoughts. You can decide to have a good attitude regardless of exterior circumstances or how other people behave.

This concept is very important, because most people wait for the outside to be perfect in order to have a good attitude and be happy[28]. This would mean that all exterior circumstances and all of the people around you, would need to be the way you want for you to be happy. This is not the way the universe

---

28 Rhonda Byrne, Hero Audio Book, Cd 2

works. If that were possible, it would compromise other people's free will and you would need to be in control of everything and everybody.

When you have positive and constructive thoughts, always expecting the best to happen, you change your beliefs and your attitude from inside out, independent of exterior circumstances or other people's behavior.

Your mind is so powerful that just by changing your thoughts, the energy that you will project to the world will change too, and people will feel it. Your powerful mind has the ability to materialize your thoughts.

All you Lived until Now is a Reflection of your Deep Beliefs

When I first listened to this statement on the program "The Awakening Course" by Dr. Joe Vitale[29], I thought, "how can I reflect a sickness? Or something really bad in my life? I surely don't want to be sick or have a bad experience."

Remembering and analyzing my life until that moment, I understood that this was absolutely true. For years, I feared being operated on for appendicitis and that is exactly what happened! I was raised believing that my body and my health were weak,

---

29 Joe Vitale, The Awakening Course, 2010

scared about cancer and, of course, while I maintained that belief, my health was bad. It got so bad that during my first pregnancy, I developed a tumor in 2005. Fortunately, my son was born through C-section and my doctor found the tumor and saw that it could be removed.

The first time I had my newborn in my arms was so touching for me that I knew I could do anything for him. What I didn't know was that life had a big trial waiting for me. Two days after the C-section, my doctor revealed something that changed my story; the tumor was ovarian cancer and it was in phase 3.

He couldn't tell me how much time I had left, or if I could survive. Of course that was shocking and right after that bitter disclosure, my husband and my mother had to travel for almost two hours to pick my father up from the airport. My son was their first grandchild; they were excited and wanted to visit us to stay for some time. All that joy that we thought was coming after having our child, in a second, was converted into the most painful sadness we could feel as a family. I didn't know what to do.

As soon as they left, I was holding my son in my arms and I made him a promise. "I promise you that I will do everything I need to do to survive and raise you." And so it was. At that time, I knew nothing about alternative medicine so I followed the traditional medicine and endured a horrible chemotherapy treatment with its devastating effects. I have to acknowledge that I was blessed with very good doctors that helped me and cared for me as a human being, not just as a patient. I am still grateful for them, as it was so hard.

Nevertheless, I focused on my promise and held onto it. I was determined to survive, and despite all the pain and obstacles that were presented, *I truly believed I could recover from it.* Plus, I had the desire to live. I didn't allow myself to give up; that was not an option for me. After a long process, the cancer was in remission.

Later, I started to do research about healthy food and alternative medicine to apply those new concepts into my family life. Certainly my health was better, but I don't consider that I was precisely the model of a healthy person. For 7 more years, I struggled with what I thought was bad luck or something unfortunate that was out of my control.

It wasn't until I started to listen to self-help programs, and applied what I learned, that I realized I was in control. Today, my son is almost 10 years old and I have no signs of cancer. In fact, I am healthier than ever!

What changed? Why am I no longer sick?

I changed my thoughts and then I changed my beliefs.

Beforehand, I believed I was weak and powerless, incapable of controlling my health and body.

Now, I know I have control over them. Even more, I can control my life, because I can choose my thoughts.

The Way Our Thoughts Are Programmed

When we listen to statements like "what you see outside is a reflection of your inside," we think it is our fault.

It is not our fault; it is our creation.

We create every day with our thoughts. In fact, what we experience today is the result of our thoughts and beliefs two or three months ago[30].

There was a time when, based on what I had experienced, I truly believed I could never be happy. Thoughts like:

- I am not pretty enough.
- I am too fat.
- I am too short.
- I am not worthy of love.
- Who's going to love me?
- I am not good enough.
- What if my destiny is to be sick?
- I am too slow.
- I have bad luck.
- Nobody will like me as I am.
- I am too fragile and weak.
- I have to be perfect to be loved.

---

30 Dawn Clark, Essential Upgrade for Money and Success Program 2014 Coaching Call 5

And I could continue with endless examples, but you get the point. Those thoughts were taking me to deep pain and desperation; I felt trapped. Thoughts like that only attract exactly what I was focusing on: suffering and misery. The fact is that none of those thoughts were true; they were just beliefs, very limiting beliefs. And on top of that, those thoughts led me to suffer with no real reason.

Reflecting and pondering about our lives with a very close friend, she said, "I agree with the fact that we create our reality, I just have a question, what happens with women that are raped? Did they want to attract that into their lives?"

I had the opportunity to have conversations with women that unfortunately had that particular experience in their lives, and the answer was very clear to me; of course they didn't want to be raped. They just had fear, a terrible fear that something like that could happen to them. Not every day did they focus on those thoughts but the fear was inside them at all times without them noticing it.

Whatever we focus our attention on tends to manifest in our lives.

The Good News is that You Can Drastically Change your Reality for Good

You may think, "if that would be so easy, there would be no suffering in the world." Well, I am here to tell you that I am living proof that although it requires changes, in essence, it is simple, better yet, possible.

Let me ask you:

- Are you ready to stop your emotional pain?
- Will you believe me when I tell you that you can find love and happiness?
- Are you willing to take the steps required to change your reality?
- Are you ready to live your best life ever?

If your answer is yes to any of these questions, congratulations! You are ready to commit to yourself to transforming your life and I can assure you, by personal experience, that this is a no-return journey. It requires a lot of courage to dare to defy your beliefs and to start inquiring why you think the way you think. Yet, in that moment, you know you are doing the right thing.

> "You are born believing in yourself, and if you are not believing in yourself now, it is because other people planted those thoughts in your mind, and you believed them."[31]

It took years of reinforcing the messages that you need to be perfect and that you are not good enough. Those messages are not true; we just believe they are true, and they hurt. Today, you can believe

---

31 Rhonda Byrne, Hero Audio Book, Cd 2

another truth. You can reprogram your mind the way you need to, and the best part is that it will take a very short amount of time.

That being said, how can we change our thoughts?

We change what we read, watch, listen to, and talk about. In other words, you change how you feed your mind with positive and empowering messages. You, and only, you decide what you think, see, watch, listen, and speak of.

If you really want to succeed in transforming your reality, and I know you do, you need to make adjustments to your lifestyle.

Until now, everything you tried didn't work, so it is time to try new things!

Start reading inspiring books, watch uplifting movies, or listen to music that will leave you a good message. Try listening to audios that will help you in personal development, especially those that talk about positive things, while avoiding negative conversations or fights.

Surround yourself with people who are positive and really care for you. Invest time in yourself, meditate, dream and enjoy life.

Look for activities that make you happy, and please switch off the radio, TV, computer, or whatever makes you feel down. Take out any negative thing and refuse to see more negative news; you have already had enough drama in your life. It is time to look for the beauty that surrounds you and to focus on the positive. Stop and smell the roses!

Stop the Pain Instantly

You are in control of your thoughts and beliefs.

What would happen if I could give you a magical wand that could make the emotional pain within you disappear? Would you grab the wand? Would you use it? If I give you the formula to ease your suffering, would you follow it?

In the numerous times that I was in desperation and I felt my heart was tearing apart, I would have reached out and would have done whatever it took to stop that suffering.

During those times, your family and close friends don't know what to do, and they just hope those feelings would pass as quickly as possible. They try to cheer you up by saying things like "this will pass," "there are worse problems in life," "this is nothing compared to what you will face later in life," "be strong and hang on," or "at your age, this is very common, you will be fine."

They say these with the best intentions in mind, but these don't help at all.

What Makes you Suffer are Your Own Thoughts about the Situation

Now, I understand what was happening. I was a victim of my thoughts, because it wasn't what happened or the facts that made me suffer; it was the meaning and importance I gave to situations[32]. Basically, what made me suffer were my own thoughts about the situations.

Especially when you are feeling sad, worried, angry, or frustrated, you can control your beliefs. The worst thing you can do is go to your room with your best collection of nostalgic and sad songs and remember a broken relationship, a painful experience or wonder why you can't find happiness.

What makes us suffer is not the facts or the things that happened. What makes us suffer is what we think about what happens.

The Magical Wand

The solution is to immediately shift your thoughts and beliefs[33]. The way a remote control changes channels in your TV (that literally is a frequency changer), is the same way you can shift your thoughts. Basically, you need to choose to change them.

---

32 Sonia Ricotti, Unsinkable program. Session 3

33 Rhonda Byrne, Hero Audio Book Cd 2

How to change your beliefs?

Think the opposite of what you were thinking, and believe that you can do it.

Then, how can you take control of your thoughts and beliefs?

Let me tell you step by step what I do.

Step 1. When you catch yourself thinking negatively, be glad that you could recognize that you are suffering for your thoughts. Feel appreciation for yourself for recognizing that.

Step 2. Right after recognizing that you are thinking out of negative beliefs, you need to act. This is very important. The quickest way to change your thoughts is by changing your environment. For example, if I am at home, I go out, even if that means just stepping out of the house to the front entrance or the backyard. If I am out of my home, I return home.

Here are the best ways to shift your thoughts; they work every time:

- Look at the sky and breathe deeply. Go out and feel the sunlight, if it is still daytime. Observe the clouds' shapes and the exquisite colors in the background. Take a deep breath and relax for a moment, or as much time as possible. If it is night, just look for the clouds or the stars. They remind us that there is a whole universe out there with endless planets and unknown worlds. Likewise, it reminds us that we are more than just flesh and bones and that our potential is limitless. Even if you are an indoor person like me, this one works really well.

- Go swimming. If you love water, this is probably your best alternative. It is so relaxing to just float and feel the water around you, leaving behind all that bothers you. Here, it's just you and the water. Also, you will spend a good amount of energy swimming, and your mind and body will release all that is hurting you.

- Help somebody. I know this one sounds odd. Have you ever helped somebody without expecting anything in return? Well, let me tell you that it is a wonderful sensation when you feel useful. That only fact changes your perspective about the situation that is bothering you. Here is the explanation: When we help somebody, usually that person is dealing with more difficult times than we are, and just by being there showing support, it make us see our challenges from a different point of view. Most of the time, our problems will seem smaller after that.

- More ideas are presented at the end of this chapter. You can combine as many of them as you feel or use just one.

Step 3. Once you feel better, write down the beliefs that made you feel bad. Start analyzing one by one, and for each one, write exactly the opposite, using positive words[34].

For instance, if I analyze this negative belief:

I never have time for myself.

The opposite will be (positive thought):

I always have time for myself.

Another example could be:

Negative belief:

Life is hard.

The opposite (positive) is:

Life is easy.

Step 4. Read the positives out loud and repeat them in your mind several times a day or every time you catch your mind going back to the initial negative thoughts. Think about these positive new beliefs right before sleep.

Do this daily with any negative belief you find, and you will see how, little by little, your mind will be programed with a new set of beliefs that empower you toward a new life.

---

34 Rhonda Byrne, Hero Audio Book, Cd 2

To Reprogram your Subconscious Mind

1. Relax and clear your mind in order to implant new thoughts. Choose the thoughts you want to implant. Think of them right before to sleep.

2. Visualize. Success is achieved twice. Make a dream book, a dream board or a dream movie.

Ideas to Uplift Energy:

- Listen to music that relaxes and inspires you.
- Drink a cup of herbal tea that enhances your mood.
- Go out and feel the sunlight. Look at the sky.
- Go out with a friend, talk, laugh a lot.
- Read a good book.
- Help somebody.
- Take a bubble bath.
- Go swimming.
- Meditate. At the beginning, I recommend doing guided meditations. You can find several. The ones I started with were the ones included in the Unsinkable Program[35].

---

35 Sonia Ricotti, Unsinkable Program, AM Morning Activations, PM Evening Activations and Self Awakening Meditations.

- Try aromatherapy.
- Connect with nature.
- Learn about a topic that you really like.
- Go to a museum.
- Take a class about something that you enjoy.
- Go to the park and observe the flowers.
- If you enjoy gardening, cultivate some flowers.
- Watch good movies. Inspiring or hilarious ones are the best.
- Go to a pet store. There, you can feel animal energy. If you love pets and you can take care of one, take the opportunity to enjoy the love of an animal. It is a different, yet pure kind of love, a never ending source of joy and love.
- Take a walk.
- Exercise.
- Run.
- Get a massage.
- Look for beauty around you.
- If you like photography, go out and take some pictures.

9

Power 4: The Power of Words You can create your new reality

"People may hear your words, but they feel your attitude"

—-John C. Maxwell: American author, speaker, and pastor

Keep Your Language Clean

This concept is beautifully explained in the book "The Four Agreements" from Don Miguel Ruiz[36]. We are the only species on Earth that can speak. Our words are very powerful; they are like magic. They have the

---

36 Don Miguel Ruiz, *The Four Agreements* 1997 The First Agreement.

power to construct or destruct, especially within ourselves.

Words create our life and make a difference whether we can or can't do something. Words create emotions within us and people around us. We also use our language everyday carelessly; once we say something, we can't go back. We can apologize, but what was said, was said. However, the person that we mostly use our words against is ourselves.

I know a woman who is brilliant, but for all of her life, she considered herself as "useless" and lived under that "hypnotic trance." When she was 8 years old, her mother left her watching her baby brother on the second floor of the house while she was cooking on the first floor. The girl was vacuuming the carpet while the baby was on the bed playing. Suddenly, when she looked back to the baby, he was on the edge of the bed. She ran to catch him, but he fell to the floor and hit his head with a scale that was under the night table. When the mother heard the baby crying and the loud sound of the fall, she immediately went up and checked on the baby. Fortunately, the baby was fine. The girl was super scared and shaking though. The mother, who was very frustrated and angry (I guess she was angrier at herself than with the girl), said to her, "you are so useless, I will tell your father, so he severely punishes you. You can't do anything right." That's it. She believed that she was useless and couldn't do anything right. She spent her youth feeling useless despite the wonderful grades she had at school and all of her efforts to choose right and to be a good support to her family.

If we could realize how strong the influence and power of our words were, maybe we'd be more careful choosing them, especially when we are angry. It is better to calm down before speaking because we can usually end up hurting the ones we love the most.

I discovered how the words I choose now have created a new relationship with myself, my family, and with people I am in contact with.

We can say words like "love" or "hate" and those two will have a completely different effect. In fact, nowadays, science has demonstrated that words, music, pictures, and prayers can shape water crystals.

Words Shape Water

Dr. Masaru Emoto[37] demonstrated how words, music, pictures, and prayers have a transforming effect in water crystals. His inspiration was to know that no two snowflakes had identical shapes. He observed the crystals of frozen water after showing letters to water, showing pictures to water, playing music to water and praying to water. He photographed the crystals and they were beautiful when water was exposed to good words, pictures, music, and prayers. However, when exposed to the contrary, the crystals were disfigured.

---

37 Dr. Masaru Emoto, http://www.masaru-emoto.net/english/water-crystal.html

Science now knows that the human body is between 50% to 78% water, depending on age and other factors. This means that at least half of our body is water. Do you realize the effects words have on you? Can you have the awareness of what you are exposing your body to every single day when you choose to see, listen, or say something negative or sad?

Almost every successful person starts their day with a positive message, and that is extremely important when they are not feeling at their best. It is like taking a daily vitamin. You don't catch them watching anything destructive. They take care of their bodies and their minds because they know that negativity only brings more negativity. In fact, most of them don't even watch the news. That doesn't mean they live completely uninformed, if there is something really big, they will certainly know it one way or the other. What that means is that they carefully choose to watch what builds them up and not otherwise.

The Power of Words

Every time we speak, we are creating and decreeing; that happens whether we want it to or not.

Once, there was a woman who was riding the bus, and she was in a wheelchair. Since she was on the bus, she constantly said every 5 minutes, "I'm scared, I'm scared! Oh my gosh, it is so difficult to be handicapped, I'm scared!" What do you think happened every time she said that? She was more scared! Of course, without knowing it, she was asking for more of that.

If we say, "life is so hard, I'm tired of this misery!" or "I don't have money, I don't know how I am going to pay my bills," each time we say it, life is harder and money is more scarce because it is what we are focusing on that we are creating.

On the other hand, if we say, "Life is easy," I can assure you that everything will be easier for you. It works like magic! Your day will be full of good things, your life will transform day by day and will be easier.

When You Talk to Yourself

When we speak to ourselves, we are being our own hypnotist, and the only ones who can break the hypnotic state are ourselves[38]. That explains why when we say "I can" or "I can't," either way, we are right.

It is really important, especially when you talk about you, or to yourself, to treat yourself as you would treat your best friend. We dearly love our best friend, and we would never say to them mean things like "idiot," "you are so stupid," "you should know that by now," "what were you thinking?" "you look awful," "who do you think you are...?", etc.

---

38 Paul Scheele, Abundance for Life Main Course, Prelude Sessions, Audio 1 Introduction 1, You, the Hypnotist.

Now, if for some reason that is the way your "best friend" treats you, it is time to rethink that relationship.

People who really care about you are the most uplifting ones, because they love you just the way you are. They are constantly recognizing your talents, virtues, and your infinite potential, even or especially those that you can't see.

Start by being *kind* to yourself. I know there are times when you wish you could have done things differently. This is where you need to remember:

What would I say to a friend in this situation? Perhaps what comes to your mind will be, "this is a learning experience. Next time, you will handle it in a different way!" or "it is ok, you don't need to be perfect every single time you try something."

We are all learning in all areas. We can learn (and I am planning to) literally until the day we die, because there's so much to explore in this marvelous universe. Be patient with yourself and try to focus on your little successes rather than on your mistakes. Celebrate your success even if they are little, because they bring you closer to your happiness.

Speak with Affirmations

Always express in a positive way. For example:

"I don't want to be sick" vs "I want to be healthy"

They express the same idea but the first sentence is formulated from a negative premise. On the other hand, the second one clearly expresses your intention with an affirmation. When we use a negative construction for a sentence, even though we say "no..." or "I don't want...," our focus is on what we don't desire for us, and we attract more of that.

There was a time when I was so sick and when I prayed, I said, "Please, I don't want to be sick." You can guess the result. Since I focused on the word sick, it was exactly what I attracted. Now I pray while saying, "Thank you, because I am healthy." Since I made that change in my language, my health is very good. I am now actually healthier than ever!

Every time you declare something, focus on it and believe it, it will manifest into your life.

Words are so powerful that simply by saying "yes," "love," or "everything it is going to be fine," you allow good things to come and manifest into your life.

So, from now on, practice to express and declare what you want with affirmations.

Avoid Negative Conversations, Complaints, and Gossip

This is a big one, especially since the world around us is full of those. Every place we turn around, there is somebody complaining, talking negative about something they dislike, or gossiping. With the news, the radio, internet, and social media, it seems like people nowadays enjoy all that negativity. We lose great energy when we get involved in those situations.

I realize that we can't control other people's words, but we can control ours. For me, I have enough with my life's challenges, and most of the time when people ask me why I don't want to know or intervene about a particular situation or conflict, I usually say:

"First, nobody asked my opinion. Secondly, it is not my business or my life. Thirdly, I can't do anything to change it."

It is amazing the amount of problems I have avoided just by not asking about other people's business. Sometimes, they come to me to tell me bad things about other people and my only answer is:

"Really, that is sad" or "I am sorry to hear that."

I don't ask more, nor do I give them any more reasons to keep talking badly. That has saved me more than once from getting involved in big gossip that only leads to suffering, drama, and tears.

To wrap up with a positive message:

Words are powerful; use them wisely and in a positive manner, focusing on what you desire in your life.

10

Power 5: The Power of Focus Declutter your life

"There is only one way to happiness and that is to cease worrying about things which are beyond the power of our will."

– Epictetus: Greek Stoic Philosopher

Remove from Your Life what is not Working

In order to move on, we need to let go of our "heavy baggage." How easy is it for you to move and walk with very heavy luggage? Not easy at all! In fact, it seems heavier with every step we take.

Can you imagine walking with that heavy luggage for years? Just thinking about it is annoying!

However, we all do carry an emotional heavy load for a long time without realizing it. Over time, we all experience deep pain in some situations and that causes emotional bruises and injuries on us. Since we don't know how to recognize we are hurt[39], those bruises and injuries become big wounds that cause emotional pain every time they are touched. In the end it is like we "add venom" to the wound, and it becomes worse with time.

The only way to heal those emotional wounds is to let go of the pain with its "venom." That means releasing those hard feelings that are causing us pain and that includes using forgiveness.

Let Go of the Need to Control

Dr. William Glasser said, "the only person whose behavior we can control is our own." This is his first Axiom in his "Choice Theory," and it really is that way.

He discovered:

> "Unlike all other living creatures, only human beings are genetically driven by the need for power. We try to satisfy that need by using what he calls, external control psychology –literally trying to force people to do what we want them to do[40]."

---

39 Don Miguel Ruiz, The Mastery of Love, 1999 Chapter 1: The Wounded Mind.

40 Dr. William Glasser, The William Glasser Institute_ http://www.wglasser.com/the-glasser-approach

This struggle has led to symptoms like depression, anxiety, bipolar disorder, anorexia, bulimia, and most emotional illnesses we see in our society or in our own homes.

Let's think about this for a second. Most of us have tried, or are still trying, to control people around us. We have the best intentions in the world and think what we want for them is the best they could be, do, or have. That is according to "our truth." Do we remember that we are starring in our own movie? And that person has the right to star in his/her own movie too? Generally, we can't see it and most of our problems and suffering originates in this fact. Each one of us has a truth and purpose and we need to let them achieve what they are born to do.

We need to accept that we can't control other people's behavior.

Deepak Chopra[41] says it is difficult enough to change a behavior in ourselves to make us happy. It is nearly impossible to change other people's behavior to make us happy.

Don't you think we have enough work to do within ourselves to, on top of that, try to "fix" other people the way we want them to be?

We can't, and we shouldn't, mess with other people's free will. Focus on helping yourself and trying to mas-

---

41 Arielle Ford, The Art of Love Relationship Series 2014

ter your mind. You will see that your life will become happier.

Let go of The Need to Be Right

When we were taught right from wrong, we were told that we need to choose the right choice, and it is true. However, we were also taught that when we choose wrong, we will be punished. We could understand two opposites; good or bad, right or wrong, white or black. We couldn't see that in between opposites were other options. For instance, that between white and black, there are many shades of gray. In our little minds, we trusted what adults told us and we believed that they didn't make mistakes, that adults were perfect.

That way of thinking is the root of the necessity to be perfect. We figured that we are either perfect or a complete disaster, that if we are not right, we are totally wrong. That is the reason why it is so painful to be "less than perfect."

As adults, it is so painful to recognize that somebody else is right[42]. Our pride and shame prevent us from recognizing that in public, even to the point that when we feel we are wrong, we still deeply defend our position because it is so important for us to "win." We will do anything to hear, "you are right, I was wrong."

---

42 Don Miguel Ruiz, *The Four Agreements, 1997* Chapter 1 Domestication and the Dream of the Planet.

Have you ever considered that any challenge has more than one way to be solved? Our universe is infinite, the possibilities and answers to issues and questions are several. It is just our belief system that sees only one way to solve them. Then, if there is more than one way to work out a situation, and more than one answer, why do we feel that only *our* point of view, *our* answer, is correct and others are wrong? And in order to "win," we can involve ourselves in endless fights and struggles? Isn't that behavior odd?

The good news is that we are not little children anymore, and we have the ability to defy the beliefs that make us suffer. One of those beliefs is that *we will dishonor ourselves if we recognize a mistake,* when it is totally the opposite. When we are able to see where and what our errors are, we have already solved half of the problem. Once we identify that we made a mistake, we can correct it. If not, we will never face it, nor fix it.

We don't need to have the right answer all the time or have the perfect solution to a problem. That is not something to be ashamed of. We can open our minds and see more than only one way to work out an issue. When we join our efforts with other people, better things happen than just one person looking for the solution.

Have you ever thought that they could be teaching you something?

Someone could say, "What can he teach me? I am more educated than him!"

Certainly, I am not talking about academic knowledge. I am talking about life knowledge and wisdom. Ultimately, this person can be teaching you how to be more humble. Life is a complex and wonderful journey. *Notice I said complex, not difficult.*

Why do we fight for "our truth" like we are in a war, attacking everyone that doesn't think like us?

Why do we think, "If he isn't with me, he is against me!"?

Why is it that we are convinced we own the one and only truth?

Do we realize that we live in an infinite universe? Some scientists are even talking about the possibility of a multiverse, more than one universe. Can you imagine the endless possibilities for everything?

And here we are, trying to say to every person that we are right and they are wrong! That attitude leads only to one feeling: suffering.

Remember, let go of the need to be right.

Let Go of the Victim Within

According to Dr. Joe Vitale,[43] this is the first level of awakening that comes with us since we were born. As infants, we didn't take responsibility of our actions

---

43 Joe Vitale, The Awakening Course, 2010

and we assumed that all that happens to us is somebody else's fault. As we grow up, we still behave like victims. We tend to blame people around us, the economy, the traffic, the weather, the government, bad luck, and everything under the sun to avoid facing that we are completely responsible for what occurs in our lives.

For example, if I can't finish a report for my boss, I will justify that with a terrible migraine, an emergency, or whatever comes to my mind to hide my responsibility for not having the report ready. The damage here is that since I don't take responsibility on it, I won't do anything to change it the next time. In fact, I will believe that there is nothing I could do to make the report on time.

The victim has an excuse or somebody to blame for every hard situation. Sadly, there are people that will die with a lot of resentment and grief, believing that they were very unfortunate in life. They behave that way, because it is too painful for them to recognize a mistake. Therefore, in their world, they really are the victims, and they suffered very deeply, because of the unfair and miserable life they were given. Their world is a valley of tears that has been controlled and ruled by somebody else, and there is nothing they can do to change it. Most of the time, they draw attention for their diseases, fears, and dramas. Victims are complaining all the time, and their lives become more and more tragic every time they make an inventory of their misadventures. They also take everything very seriously and personally. For them, all is a tragedy.

After I recognized that I was behaving like a victim, I took responsibility for the things I could change, and then I laughed. Laughing about situations makes facts less tragic, so we can relax, breathe, and analyze the challenge and then find the solution.

Once I brought this victim concept to my family, every time we found any of us acting like a victim, we would say, "Do you want me to play the violin for you?" And the person recognizes his/her behavior and replies, "Yes, please." After that, we all laugh. We don't make fun of each other with the intention to hurt anybody's feelings; *we just laugh at how dramatically we display the situations*. Lately, we have been adding the TNT channel slogan, *"We know drama,"* and in no time, everybody is laughing and hugging the person that was previously feeling down.

Of course, there are situations where we know it is a painful one, so we respect the other person's feelings. When the crisis is over, we can talk about that and be supportive with each other. After all, that is what family is about: support and love.

When we are in victim mode, we can't take control of our lives, we can't create our own path, nor can we reach our goals. Then, we feel completely powerless. The good news is that we can choose.

We can choose to be the victim, or we can choose to be the active writer and protagonist of our lives.

Let Go of the Past. Live in the Present

When we live attached to the past, we miss our present. The worst thing is that we can feel all the regret in the world about a situation, and yet, there is nothing we can do to change it. We can't go back to the past and change it, not even a second of it. The "if I had…" doesn't exist. We will never know what would have happened "if I had…" It is just a waste of energy; energy that we need to change our future.

We all have situations when we wish, "if I had done…, then…" or "if I had said…, then …"

I still have them now and then. However, now I know I can choose to feel guilty and torment myself about a mistake or learn from it and do it better next time. *It is my choice.*

It is important to live in the present. We call it the *present*, because it is a gift. Today, we can make choices. Today, we can fix things to have a better future, to create the lives we want for ourselves.

Today, we can choose to be happy or to continue crying for the past and ruin our future.

Let Go of the Mistakes: Healing Through Forgiveness

Forgiveness is, maybe, the hardest thing to do, however, it is the only way to truly move on. I am talking about real forgiveness; the kind of forgiveness that means you can talk or even hug the person that offended you.

There is one trap though. Sometimes, we don't have any problem forgiving other people, yet we feel it is impossible to forgive one person; ourselves.

Forgiving Ourselves

We feel so unintelligent, ashamed, or stupid about our actions that it is nearly impossible to forgive ourselves.

Feelings of regret are very common any time things don't come out as we expected. We blame ourselves like the worst Judge and condemn ourselves with the hardest punishments possible.

This feeling is always "after the fact."[44] What we don't realize is that now we have more knowledge and elements to evaluate the situation than we had at the time the mistake occurred.

---

44 Paul Scheele, Ultimate You Mindfest, Audio Set 6: Feel Great About Yourself. http://www.learningstrategies.com

Regrets come, because we would have handled things differently if we knew what we know now. If you think about it, it is very unfair to treat yourself badly because, at that time, you didn't know it. You did the best you could with the elements you had.

When we understand that, it is easier to forgive ourselves. Again, treat you as you would treat your best friend. Be patient with yourself, recognize the good things you have done and stop wondering "if I had..."

Decide to look to your present and what you can do different TODAY to have a different outcome TOMORROW.

Forgive Other People

For most of us, it is very difficult to forgive other people. We yield to the temptation to think that not forgiving gives us power over the other person. That is a mistake. Actually, that is *our* mistake. We think it is our "secret weapon," thus every time we are arguing with this person, especially if we are "losing the battle," we "unsheathe our sword" and attack directly to the heart, remembering that person's unforgivable error. Thereby, we feel we won and enjoy our victory... is that really a victory? After all that energy drainage, there are no winners. In fact, everybody is even more hurt, therefore, we all lose.

You see, when we hold resentment, hatred, and all those emotions towards another person, it is like drinking venom yourself and expecting the other person to die poisoned. The only person dying is you!

Please don't misunderstand what I am telling you:

- I am not asking you to feel nothing if somebody offends you.
- I am not saying that you need to be best friend with that person.
- Forgiving other people doesn't mean you give them permission to mistreat or abuse you.

I am just saying that holding hard feelings for other people is mostly hurting ourselves. We all make mistakes; it is an important part of the learning process.

I would like to emphasize the word *holding*, and I do it for a reason. There is nothing wrong in feeling any emotion. We tend to label feelings and emotions as positive or negative, and, of course, they generate energy that is either positive or negative. But, how can we know our true desires without our emotions?

Do not feel guilty or judge yourself for experiencing negative emotions, because in order to let go and forgive, you need to come back to the situation and feel the emotions. After you feel the emotions you can learn, understand, and *then* forgive and let go.

I highlight the word *then*, because if you do not take the time to feel the emotions, process, learn, and understand them *before* you forgive and let go, you are just hiding or denying your emotions and feelings.

The thing is, those heavy emotions grow and grow with time. Sometimes, they even trigger unwanted behaviors until there is one day when you feel you can't bear it anymore and you want to explode. The problem is that the consequences of that explosion are bigger than the original issue. People involved will think you are exaggerating about it and in the end, not even you will understand what happened inside you to make you feel that overwhelming emotion. In the end, we feel guilty for our "overreaction" and for feeling overwhelmed.

Most people may think:

- What if the other person does not recognize his/her mistake?
- What if they are not repented?
- What if they don't care?
- What if they don't deserve that forgiveness from me?

My answer is this; *it doesn't matter.*

Forgiveness is the only way to free ourselves from the burden that does not allow us to move on. *Actually, forgiveness is the greatest demonstration of love for ourselves.* When we forgive, the biggest benefit is for us.

In my research, I learned that people usually do the best they can. Nobody wakes up thinking, "how can I make the most mistakes and hurt a lot of people today?" That simply is not the case.

Our nature is to give and receive love. Think about a one year old baby. She is tender, she is curious, she likes to explore the world, and she wants to learn all things. She smiles very often and enjoys hugs and love. She is not worried about the future and does not live in the past. She enjoys her present time with all of her senses. She doesn't know about resentment or how to hold hard feelings for anybody. She forgives our mistakes and we can feel it. That is our nature, how we truly are. When we grow up, everything changes and the degree of "damage" depends on how people around us behave.

The second reason to forgive is that we never know when we can hurt somebody else with or without realizing it. And, when we are in that position, we will ask for forgiveness, hoping the other person can forgive and let it go.

Allow me to add some reflections:

Have you ever considered that, in most circumstances, we feel offended because we take other people's actions personally?

Remember, every one of us is the protagonist of our own movie. Not everything people do is because of us and a lot of times, people don't even know they did something to hurt us.

The other consideration I would like to explain is that we are all different when concerning our degree of "understanding." I am not talking about intelligence, because I know we all are intelligent and perfect for our purpose here. I am talking about the "amount of truth" that people can understand. Some people carry a tremendous amount of grief due to their experiences in life. For them, facing those emotions is extremely difficult to bear. Some could even be disconnected from the real world and create their own world. It is okay, it is all the truth they can take.

After a lot of struggling, I finally found a way to see it. I think about these people like little siblings. For those of you who have younger siblings, at some point in your childhood, one of your parents told you, "You are the oldest child, you can understand things that your younger siblings can't understand yet, so please try to be more patient with them and forgive their behavior because they are little ones."

This way of seeing some people has helped me to have better relationships, less struggle, and more peace.

Embrace Change

Change is something that most of mankind resists.

We don't want changes, because they take us out of our "comfort zone." Change is inevitable. The more we resist it, the more we'll struggle. We can nag, blame, get angry, and complain "why?" as many times as we want, but nothing will be the way it used to be again. This is true for society, companies, families, relationships, and individuals.

When I look back to how I used to be and how I am now, my heart fills with a deep gratitude that I could change. I changed my thinking, my emotions, my motives, my goals, and my attitude towards life and myself. When I remember how I used to see life, I am glad I was willing to change. Otherwise, I would be making the same mistakes over and over. Overall, change is positive. It is the way we can improve; the only way to grow as human beings.

In nature, everything changes. Species evolve and even rocks are changed by erosion over hundreds of years.

If we can count on anything permanent, it is change. For that reason, embrace change!

How to Remove Unwanted Things from Your Life

Start changing your thoughts and everything else will fall into place. When you feel bad, go and do whatever makes you feel happy. If what makes you happy is to swim, go for it! If you enjoy baking cakes, do it! That automatically will shift your thoughts and bring you to a place of hope, because you will be in a state of bliss.

11

Power 6: The Power of Gratitude The Beginning of Happiness

"I have the choice to be angry at God for what I don't have or be thankful for what I do have."

—-Nick Vujicic: Author, Motivational speaker

Gratitude is the Beginning of Happiness

Gratitude is a powerful feeling. It brings you to a place where you can focus on good things, on all of the assets and miracles you have received throughout your life and all you have right now in this moment. We have a tendency to take every good thing for granted. For instance, we can drink water, we can eat, we can read; all these things are reasons to be grateful.

Have you ever been or had somebody you know in surgery? It is really frustrating when you are thirsty and hungry and you can't eat or drink, because of the surgery.

When we count our blessings, we are focusing on what we have, and it is then that we realize that we have a lot to be grateful for. When we are looking for the things we don't have, we feel empty, sad, and bitter. If we choose this attitude, we will never be satisfied with all we have, and nothing will be enough. Even if we had everything, we would feel bitter, because that is the way we would see life.

Gratitude: An Instantaneous Source of Joy

Do you want to feel instant joy? Count 5 things to be grateful for. If for some reason you can't find them, then you know your attitude is not one of gratitude. The good news is that you can choose your attitude.

Just think about these facts in your day:

- Can you walk?
- Can you read?
- Can you see?
- Do you have a family?
- Do you have friends?
- Do you have a bed?
- Do you have a place to take a shower?

- Do you have food?
- Are you healthy?
- Do you have a home?
- Do you have a car?

We can continue making lists of things to be grateful for in our lives.

Do you realize you have reasons to be grateful?

The more we recognize and feel gratitude for our current circumstances, the more reasons we will find to be grateful. I have tried it in my life and it works every time. In fact, just feeling gratitude for what it has given to us brings wonderful, unexpectedly good things into our reality.

Practice this: Every day, when you wake up, count 5 things[45] to be grateful for. Write them down. You will see more things to be grateful for every day.

Another way to go deeper into gratitude is to focus on just one thing, or person, to be grateful for. Now, write 3 or 5 details why you are grateful to have that particular blessing in your life.[46] This exercise helps us to really appreciate all the good that we usually take

---

45 Bob Proctor. Interview with Sonia Ricotti, 2014

46 Marie Forleo. http://www.marieforleo.com/2014/11/powerful-gratitude-practice/

for granted and that we only notice when it is gone, when it is too late.

Gratitude is Linked to Humbleness

In order to be grateful for something, first we need to recognize that we have received something. That simple act places us in a humble position, where we can feel appreciation for the good received. When we are truly feeling gratitude for something, there is no place for pride or arrogance. If we are grateful for a favor, service, work, help, support, or even an attitude, we will have more of what we are grateful for. As we stated before, we will attract more of what we focus on.

I understand that in some situations, extreme situations, it is complicated to be grateful for anything. There are circumstances where we feel so sad or broken that our hearts have a hard time finding reasons to be grateful. Yet, even in those situations, we can feel gratitude.

I know a man that had a situation that for anybody would be devastating. He is a single parent with five kids. That night he was going to sleep and suddenly a short circuit went under his mobile home and started a fire in one of the bedrooms. They were already sleeping when his neighbor's dog started barking. His neighbor went outside and noticed the fire. He immediately woke them up and they had to escape from the mobile home through the windows. He had no insurance. He had no money and all he had was gone. The fire was so quick that nothing could be saved. A lot of people showed up to help. Even the fire department helped with the hotel for a couple of days. When I talked to him, he was grateful because none of them had any signs of burn injuries, not a single finger! He was grateful for all the help they received and started a new life in a better place than they had before.

In the same situation, what would you choose? Be grateful for the health you still had? Or be bitter for your bad luck and losing everything?

We can always choose, it is up to you!

12

Power 7: The Power of Action Creating your Dream Life

"The best is yet to come"

– William Shakespeare: Poet

Be Brave and Change What you Can Control

You already have knowledge of what your powers are and what you can control.

Accept the fact that the only person you can control is yourself. That means that you can change many things that depend on your decisions, for example:

- Your priorities
- Your schedule
- Your appearance

- Your environment
- Your career
- Your activities

Reclaim your Power

By exercising your freedom to choose, you are reclaiming your power. Now you are aware of the steps to take to be in harmony with the person you really are, while being aligned with your own core values and what you want for your life. The only one who can set you free from your old thoughts and suffering is you.

Steps to Happiness

1. **Use the power of clarity:** Discover what you want: Be honest and true to yourself. What makes you happy? What is your heart telling you?
2. **Use the power of choice:** Take responsibility and ownership of your free will. Every day, every time, we can always choose. You will face the consequences of your actions anyway, so choose your life, learn and enjoy it.
3. **Use the power of your thoughts:** Your thoughts are energy, and they vibrate in frequencies. You can choose your thoughts that form your beliefs, attitude, and paradigms.

Thoughts generate feelings. There's a law that independently of the fact that you believe it or not, works all the time: You attract what you focus on.

4. **Use your magical wand:** Shift your thoughts. You are in control of them. Choose wisely what you watch, listen, and say. Stay on the positive side.
5. **Use the power of your words:** Your words have the power to create or destroy. Choose carefully what you say to your loved ones and especially to yourself. Speak with affirmations. Treat yourself as you would treat your best friend.
6. **Use the power of focus:** *Focus on what you want and remove what is not working:* You can remove from your life what is holding you back. Let go of the need to control everything and everybody. Let go of the need to be right. Let go of your past and live in the present. Forgive yourself and forgive other people. We need to forgive, because it is the only way we can be free. *Forgiveness is the greatest demonstration of love for ourselves.* Embrace change. How can you do all this? Change your thoughts!
7. **Use the power of gratitude:** Gratitude is the beginning of happiness and gives you instant joy. It is important to be grateful, especially when things are not going your way. Count 5

things to be grateful for every day. Focus on one thing or person you are grateful for, and think about 3 or 5 details as to why you appreciate having them in your life. Be grateful for all you have; that attitude will attract more wonderful things into your life.

8. **Use the power of action:** You need to take action in order to transform your reality. Start with baby steps. Keep going and be patient with yourself. Celebrate your success. Pay attention to things you are doing better and do more of them. Every day, do something that makes you happy, as little as it may be; that will leave you with a good attitude.

Enjoy the New You

You have worked so hard to be on the path of happiness, that it is time to enjoy the new person you are, the "new you."

Sometimes, it seems like we make no progress. Still, something inside us is transforming. The day will come when you look back and see how much you have evolved. You will see how different you are now.

Every person has their own talents, gifts, and virtues. No one is exactly the same, not even identical twins; their talents and personalities are completely different. You are unique and came to Earth with a mission. Of course, the more we cultivate our virtues and talents, the happier we will be and the more probabilities we will have to attract happiness.

I know somebody will think, "what if I really don't like something about myself and that makes me unhappy?" Well, in that case, you are in control of your body and your mind. Therefore, *you have the power to change it.* It is your choice.

Do these Every Day

- Be patient with yourself. When we start learning something, we will make mistakes; that is how it works. It takes time to master any skill.
- Be true to yourself. When you don't feel like doing anything other people ask you to do, don't do it. You don't need to please everybody all the time.
- Surround yourself with positive people; they will be an excellent support system for your journey.
- If you are going to wonder, do it to the positive outcome.
- Laugh more.
- Try to balance your activities.
- Do your best every day.
- Do not overdo it.
- The more you recognize you are in control of your reality, the more it will be like you want.

- Think of every difficult situation as a challenge and not as a tragedy so that it is easier to find a solution.

Learn to recognize what you can control –the only person you can control is yourself – and what you can't. For the ones you can't control, trust they will be solved one way or the other.

Freedom Day: Choose your Happiness

There is nothing more exciting than the feeling of freedom and that you enjoy being yourself.

When I started to love me, my freedom, and the time I spent with myself, for the first time I could feel happy about myself. In that very moment is when everything changed: Even though my life is not perfect, I can still feel peace, I can feel love for the person I am, and at the same time I can feel people's love.

I am in control of my mind and body. I am creating the reality I truly want for me and exercising my power of controlling my thoughts, feelings, words, and actions. Thereby, I am on my way to achieving all my dreams and to manifesting all that I want in my life.

It doesn't matter where you are in your life right now, what happened to you, any mistake you made, or how worthless you feel. I invite you to live the life you came here to live.

How am I so certain you can do it? Because I did it, and if I can do it, then everybody can do it!

There are only two requirements to do it: desire and willpower.

If you desire to be free and happy, then you will find the determination to do whatever it takes to accomplish it.

I am here to urge you to find your real purpose in life. Please don't delay the necessary steps to heal yourself. Get up and move on to that wonderful and exciting world that is waiting for your gifts! Bring out that magnificent being that you are and shine!

And remember, the best is yet to come!

****

Want more?

YOU MADE IT and are officially ready to use your 7 mind powers to achieve happiness!

I am very grateful that you took the time to read this, so I wanted to give you a special gift. If you want free access to an eBook that is related to this topic, more information, content to improve yourself and live the life or your dreams, make sure to participate in my email list, where I share my favorite tips on how to achieve happiness one step at a time.

Here is the link to access and get the eBook for free

http://www.MindfulnessHappiness.com

– Paola

Founder of Mindfulness and Happiness Movement

Bibliography

1, 22 William Glasser, M.D., *Choice Theory*. New York: HarperCollinsPublishers, Inc 1998

3, 36, 42 Don Miguel Ruiz, *The Four Agreements*. California: Amber-Allen Publishing, Inc 1997

7, 39 Don Miguel Ruiz, *The Mastery of Love*. California: Amber-Allen Publishing, Inc 1999

17, 28, 31, 33, 34 Rhonda Byrne, *Hero Audio Book (The Secret Series)* Simon & Schuster Audio; Unabridged edition 2013

Programs and Websites

1, 23, 40 The William Glasser Institute
http://www.wglasser.com/the-glasser-approach

2, 41 Arielle Ford, The Art of Love Relationship Series 2014
http://elevate.us/art-of-love-relationship-series-with-arielle-ford-deepak-chopras-4-simple-steps-to-deeper-intimacy/

4 Jennifer McLean 13th volume, Healing with the Masters.
http://healingwiththemasters.com

5 Hugo, 2011
http://www.paramountmovies.com/hugomovie.html

6 The Missing Secret Program, Joe Vitale
https://www.nightingale.com/products/missing-secret/

8, 14, 27 Loral Langemeier and Bob Proctor, Expression of your Power. Live out Loud- Expression vs. Suppression
http://liveoutloud.com/product/expression-of-your-power/

9 http://josefeliciano.com/wp/faqs

10 http://www.lifewithoutlimbs.org/about-nick/bio

11 http://www.attitudeisaltitude.com/about-nick-his-story

12 http://www.goodreads.com/author/quotes/3395320.nick_vujicic

13 Utah FosterCare, *On Becoming a Foster Parent Manual,* Developed by *The Institute for Human Services, June 2001 Updated February 2014* http://utahfostercare.org/

15 http://www.automaticincomecoach.com/

16, 18, 26, 38 Paul Scheele, Abundance for Life Program http://www.learningstrategies.com/AbundanceForLife/Home.asp

19 Natalie Ledwell, The Inspiration Show http://www.mindmovies.com/inspirationshow/archive.php?episode=8

20, 32, 35 Sonia Ricotti, Unsinkable program, Bonus Class http://www.leadoutloud.ca/

21 http://www.how-to-change-careers.com/new-career-ideas.html

24 Mary Morrissey, Dream Builder Program http://www.dreambuilderprogram.com/registration/

25 Dr. Hans Jenny, Cymatics experiments, 1960 https://www.youtube.com/watch?v=I4jUMWFKPTY

29, 43 Joe Vitale, The Awakening Course, 2010

30 Dawn Clark, Essential Upgrade for Money and Success Program, 2014 Coaching Call 5 https://www.dawnclark.net/essential-upgrade-secret-language-of-success/

37 Dr. Masaru Emoto http://www.masaru-emoto.net/english/water-crystal.html

44 Paul Scheele, Ultimate You Mindfest, http://www.learningstrategies.com

45 Bob Proctor, Interview with Sonia Ricotti, Launch Unsinkable Program 2014

46 Marie Forleo http://www.marieforleo.com/2014/11/powerful-gratitude-practice

About the Author

PAOLA LUJAN was born in Lima, Peru. Her self-help journey started when she read "Your Erroneous Zones" by Dr. Wayne W. Dyer, when she was 12 years old. Her father enjoyed reading self-help books and she learned to love them too. Then, she read "Success through a Positive Mental Attitude," "Think and Grow Rich," and "The Master Key to Riches" by Napoleon Hill. Those inspiring books were followed by many others through her teenage years.

At that point in her life, she had a rebellious attitude towards societal rules that she considered not helpful to the development of an individuals' special talents. She always felt that there was something else in life, more meaning than just to be born, grow, go to school, go the university to have more education, get a "good job" so we can make a living until we retire, and then just "enjoy life" for a few years and wait until we die.

After graduating from High School with honors, she went to the university, as was expected of her. She graduated as an Architect and Planner in 1997. She moved to the United States and married in 2001.

During 2006 her mother sent her one of the greatest gifts of all. It was the book "The Four Agreements" by Don Miguel Ruiz. That book changed her life. It changed the way she saw life and was confirmation that she was not crazy; that more people, even ancient wisdom questioned the same things she did.

She was still "sleeping;" she was not happy with her life. Even though she knew there was something better, it seemed like it was not for her.

One day she checked out a book from a public library, "Yes! Energy" by Loral Langemeier. It opened a whole new world for her, a world where she could wonder and dream her wildest dreams with nobody to say, "That is so selfish of you", or "who do you think you are to..." or "you have to be realistic, you know".

After that book, she followed several personal development programs that helped her focused on what she really wanted to do in her life: Be an author and motivational speaker.

She is the founder of Mindfulness and Happiness Movement and also MindfulnessHappiness.com, where she plans to spread inspiration and hope to everybody that is willing to listen. She truly believes we can contribute to a better world one person at a time, especially by healing ourselves first. She feels very grateful for the life she enjoys today.

To communicate with her and receive free inspirational messages go to:

http://www.MindfulnessHappiness.com

www.ingramcontent.com/pod-product-compliance
Lightning Source LLC
Chambersburg PA
CBHW072025040426
42447CB00009B/1733